M01 40001 89762

D1074883

[

The Springer Series
on Death and Suicide

ROBERT KASTENBAUM, Ph.D., Series Editor

Richard Lonetto, Ph.D., is an associate professor of psychology at the University of Guelph in Ontario, Canada and coeditor of the journal *Essence: Issues in the Study of Aging, Dying and Death*. A graduate of the City College of New York, he received his Ph.D. from New York University. At the University of Guelph, he established one of the first courses in Canada in the psychology of death.

CHILDREN'S CONCEPTIONS OF DEATH

Richard Lonetto, *Ph.D.*

SPRINGER PUBLISHING COMPANY
New York

Springer Publishing Company, Inc.
200 Park Avenue South
New York, New York 10003

80 81 82 83 84 / 10 9 8 7 6 5 4 3 2 1

Library of Congress Cataloging in Publication Data

Lonetto, Richard.
    Children's conceptions of death.

    (Springer series on death and suicide ; 3)
    Includes bibliographical references and index.
    1. Children and death. I. Title. II. Series.
BF723.D3L66   155.4'18   79-24334
ISBN 0-8261-2550-6
ISBN 0-8261-2551-4 pbk.

Printed in the United States of America.

For
Sarin
Temujinn
and Aaron

Contents

Foreword 1

The philosopher may be regarded as a sort of *Hermes psychopompos*, accompanying his colleagues but usually not interfering with their activities. Once in a while, however, on a long journey, one may stop to rest, look backward and forward over the landscape, and try to find out where one actually is. Then the philosopher, as a friend, may also say what he sees and, perhaps, contribute to the orientation of the travelers. It is in this sense, I think, that my colleague Richard Lonetto has asked me to write a preface to his book, *Children's Conceptions of Death*. Reading it aroused a variety of associations in me; the first group was epistemological and the second one might be called metaphysical. Let me now summarize them in this sequence.

Epistemological Associations

Werner Heisenberg's uncertainty principle says, "The more exactly I determine the location of an object, the more vaguely can I indicate its motion; the more exactly I have measured an object's place and spatial structure, the less I know about its motion and vice versa."[1] Niels Bohr has made a thought-provoking attempt to apply this principle to biology, saying, "The more exactly I have measured an organism quantitatively, the less I know of it as a living, developing body. Quantifying measurement gives only insufficient information about the *bios*."[2]

In Lonetto's book I have found a passage where, it would seem, the uncertainty principle is applied to psychological phenomena, and also is implicitly applied to cultural phenomena in general:

> . . . It is not unusual to find that assessments of [children's] drawings show reasonable reliability and low validity; in fact, the more rigorously defined and controlled the study, the lower the validity, especially with respect to the development of personality . . . . [p. 50]

The drive to "rigorously define and control," which usually means to quantify everything without making exception for cultural phenomena, sometimes leads to comic enterprises. One of the deans of a North American university devised a formula whereby the teaching effectiveness of every professor could be measured objectively, which, of course, meant quantitatively! "The academic's disease in our time is the quantification itch," remarks Dr. Percy Smith, Vice-President of the University of Guelph.[3] The German philosopher Erich Rothacker never grew tired of showing that we commit a serious mistake if we believe that by using quantification and a scientific vocabulary we can ever adequately understand and describe culture. He once said that someone who called a good wine alcohol was as uncultured as someone who called his sweetheart a mammal.[4]

It may be high time indeed to apply Heisenberg's uncertainty principle, not only, as Niels Bohr suggested, to biology, but also to cultural life. We should recognize that the more exactly we have quantified a cultural phenomenon, the more we have treated it as something dead.

In all kinds of measuring we use forms of intuition (time and space) and categories (causality, quantity, and so forth). These forms are inherent in our minds and shape all our perceptions. Immanuel Kant believed that, on the one hand, as consciously thinking beings, we cannot help using these forms as tools of perception; on the other hand, we only perceive aspects of things by means of them. These aspects he calls *Erscheinungen*, and says that we do not perceive the things in themselves, because they are inaccessible. Heisenberg and many modern physicists find themselves in Kant's camp when they say that "in the act of measurement the physicist interacts with the observed object and thus causes it to be revealed not as it is in itself but as a function of measurement."[5]

The phenomenological school regards things in themselves as intentional contents of our consciousness (phenomena). They can, as such, be made accessible, describable and intersubjectively communicable. But phenomena are only accessible, phenomenologists stress, if we first of all practice suspension of judgment *(epoché);* that is, if we are silent and let the phenomena speak to us and reveal themselves to us. This is what Richard Lonetto does with children's representations of death in this book and it is why the tale of little Jennifer is found here. This book shows us both the inevitability of the use of categories, including quantity (see the questionnaire statistics), as well as their limits. The phenomena themselves must speak to us. Here the child's image and experience of death are speaking to us; we recognize that death need not be dark if love and truth unite in facing it.

Metaphysical Associations

The journey toward the origin and the limits of being is archetypal behavior. It recurs in all cultures and generations and in the life of every individual. Both Gilgamesh in the old Orient and Ulysses in Mediterranean antiquity made such a journey. In the Germanic north, Parzival and Faust did the same. Our century, too, and perhaps especially our century, has seen a variety of journeys toward the origin and limits of being. Research in micro- and macrophysics on the structure of the atom and on the genesis of our universe investigates the limits and origins of the cosmos.

Astronauts belong in this context, too. Studies of primitive tribes and of the genesis of mankind investigate the origin of the human species and of society. Frobenius and Spengler's theory about cultural circles tries to investigate the end and the dying out of cultures.

There is also a rich variety of investigations into the origins and limits of individual life; that is, of birth and childhood and of old age and death. In Switzerland, a *Psychology of the New-Born Child* has been published.[6] Indeed, even a *Society for Pre-Natal Psychology* has been founded.[7] In America, Elizabeth Kübler-Ross is studying the experiences of dying persons and their environment and in Canada, Professors Lonetto and Fleming publish the journal *Essence*, which contains studies on aging and death.[8] Both Sigmund Freud's and Carl Gustav Jung's long journeys into the depths of sick, healthy, individual, and collective psyches must be mentioned here, as well as Jean Piaget's investigation of the beginnings of knowledge in children and Szondi's analysis of destiny. In 1905 in Munich, Georg Kerschensteiner published his great study, *Die Entwicklung der zeichnerischen Begabung.* In the same year, André Derain bought African sculptures in Marseille for himself and for his friend Maurice Vlaminck.[9] Kerschensteiner, in studying children's drawings, was looking for the genesis of artistic activity in the individual; Derain, in collecting African sculptures, was looking for the beginnings of art of all mankind. The Dada movement of the second and third decade of our century tried in a practical way to go back to the beginnings of art, that is, to its elements. Writing poetry, to these people, was playing with mere sounds, painting was playing with mere colors or with objects. At the same time, Paul Klee and Wassily Kandinsky, with a more careful and conscious method than the noisy Dada crowd, pursued experiments with the pure elements of art in their Bauhaus studios.[10]

In 1900, in her book, *The Century of the Child*, Ellen Key predicted that in the coming one hundred years mankind would mainly be concerned with the child. We are aware, however, that in the second half of our century there is also a growing concern with old age and death. Thus, we might rather label our age "the century of research about extremes, origins and limits." Richard Lonetto's book on children's representations of death falls into this broad context. This work tries to investigate the frontier areas of human life in two directions: backward toward childhood and birth and forward toward old age and death. Lonetto asks how the end is mirrored in the beginning, and he finds in the small child's mind a pre-temporal and pre-causal unity of being that encompasses both life and death. Soon, however, this unity is forgotten. Temporal and causal thinking superimpose themselves on the earlier state of mind and cover it up.

This may remind us of Martin Heidegger's image of the development of Western philosophy, which seems on a larger scale to parallel the development of the child's mind as Lonetto depicts it. According to Heidegger, there was awareness of Being, of the One, in the pre-Socratic thinkers. Soon after the peak of Greek thought in Plato and Aristotle, however, "forgetfulness of Being" came about and has lasted into modern times. Now, philosophers are again trying to become aware of the One, of Being itself.[11] Lonetto's findings also remind us of the words of many poets who, throughout all the epochs, have preserved and expressed the experience of oneness. Rainer Maria Rilke in one of the prayers of his *Book of Hours*[12] says,

> Loudly you said: *Life;*
> and softly you said: *Death;*
> and again and again you repeated: *Being.*

Jakob Amstutz
Goettingen, Switzerland
March, 1979

Notes

1. Georges Matisse, *Interpretation philosophique des relations d'incertitude et du determinisme.* Paris, 1936.
2. Stefan Rozental (ed.), *Niels Bohr. His life and work as seen by his friends*

and colleagues. Amsterdam, 1967, 92 and 308. (Bohr sometimes mentions "analogies" between principles in physics and in psychology. In particular, he expanded his principle of complementarity into a universally valid principle, and chose as motto for his coat of arms "Contraria sunt complementa." This is also the principle of individuation for C.G. Jung.) *See also* Walter Heitler, "Ueber die Komplementaritaet von lebloser und lebender Materie," *Scheidewege*, VIII/4, Stuttgart, 1978.

3. Percy Smith, *I Quantify Therefore I Am.* Bulletin of the Canadian Association of University Professors, Vol. 21, No. 1, October 1972, 25 to 27.

4. Erich Rothacker, *Zur Genealogie des menschlichen Bewusstseins.* Bonn, 1966, IX.

5. Iso Kern, *Husserl und Kant. Eine Untersuchung ueber Husserls Verhaeltnis zu Kant und zum Neukantianismus.* Den Haag, 1964. (Kern offers an exhaustive comparison of Kant's and Husserl's epistemology. On Heisenberg, I quote the formulation Patrick A. Heelan uses in his Encyclopedia Britannica article on the great physicist.)

6. Fritz Stirnimann, *Psychologie des neugeborenen Kindes.* Zurich, 1940.

7. Gesellschaft fur Praenatale Psychologie, founded in 1974 by Dr. Gustav Graber in Bern.

8. *See* bibliography at the end of this book.

9. André Derain, *Lettres à Vlaminck.* Paris, 1955, 185 passim.

10. Hugo Ball, "Manifest zum one. Dada-Abend." Zurich, 1916. In Paul Portner (ed.), *Literatur-Revolution 1910–1925. Dokumente, Manifeste, Programme.* Vol. 11. Neuwied, 1961. Also: Wassily Kandinsky, *Ueber das Geistige in der Kunst.* Munchen, 1911. Paul Klee, *Ueber die moderne Kunst.* Bern, 1945. (Lecture given by the artist and teacher at the opening of an exhibition of his work in Jena, 1924.) Hans Prinzhorn, *Bildnerei der Geisteskranken.* Springer Verlag, Berlin, 1923. (This, together with books on the art of children and of primitives, is another expedition toward the borderlines of human experience.)

11. Martin Heidegger, "Der Spruch des Anaximander." In *Holzwege*, Frankfurt, 1950, 296 ss, particularly 336–343. (Such representations of his image of the development of Western thought are frequent in Heidegger. In *Holzwege* 336, the following sentence is emphasized: "Forgetfulness of Being is the forgetfulness of the difference between Being and being things" [Transl. by J.A.].)

12. Rainer Maria Rilke, *Sämtliche Werke.* Frankfurt, 1955, I 257. (Transl. by J.A.)

Foreword 2

Researchers have often found that they can learn more about child development by observing the structure children impose on their environment than by imposing a structure on the child's behavior through the demands of a particular research process. Richard Lonetto's book primarily reflects the former approach. A comprehensive review of research on children's conceptions of death is included, along with findings from the research of Lonetto and his colleagues. The main emphasis, however, is a phenomenological one, which describes the child's view of death through children's words and drawings.

•Just as the child changes rapidly in most areas from birth through death, so does the child's conception of death go through comparable extensive development. Both these changes and the influences that could have caused them are discussed. It is still early in this new area to be able to conclude whether the influence on the child's ideas of death comes from maturation of cognitive abilities or from parents, schools, and other social influences. Reading the discussion of the changes that occur does provide a number of leads that will be of interest to the reader.

The author does not force the changes in the child's conception of death into a rigid ages-and-stages pattern, but describes characteristics of three "approximate age" levels. He notes the evidence that the development of the child's concepts is related to mental age or intellectual ability more than chronological age, which suggests that cognitive ability may be more closely related to the changes than is experience.

A number of aspects of a child's development begin as the child's observations of external events and become integral parts of the child's thoughts as development proceeds. Language is the best example. Lonetto points out a similar process with the child's conception of death, and he suggests several steps in language and cognitive development that may be antecedents of advances in the child's conception of death. The introduction to death for the 3-to-5-year-old is often the observation of a dead animal or the death of a relative. The preschool child's view of death from his own words or drawings seems to be a concrete view of death as quite limited in its meaning, and as reversible as the cycle of sleeping and awakening. The fear of death at this age centers on external separation from the needed parent or parents.

Within the next few years, by nine years of age, the child has come to see death as universal. By this point, and after it, children see death as a terrible thing with much more of an internal, personal relevance than was true at an earlier age. Lonetto notes many changes in social influences upon the child during the time when the child's view of death is evolving.

The author notes, "If old age *causes* death, as parents have told their children, is it any wonder that we continue to have an adult society that fears aging and cherishes youth?" The child's notion of old age causing death may be reinforced by our tendency to institutionalize the aged. At a time when gerontologists are attempting to break the stereotype we have of aging and when they are pointing out that people do not "die of old age," it is quite timely to look at this aspect of children's views. The author notes that in looking at the steps in the child's developing conception of death we also gain understanding of the background parameters of the adult's concepts of death.

In addition to every child's development of an abstract conception of death, some children experience their own impending death because of fatal illnesses, or the death of parents or siblings. The author reviews the research that is available on children's reactions to these experiences. Researchers often expected that the death of a child's parents might be related to subsequent abnormal personality development, but the review shows that there are few clearly established findings in this area.

Lonetto observes that having children play or draw death can help them cope with their fears, perhaps through making death a more tangible opponent. The author also offers a discussion and a number of guidelines to enable parents, teachers, or others to explain death to a child in an effective and helpful manner.

Marshall L. Hamilton, Ph.D.
Indio, California
August, 1979

Acknowledgments

No book is written in isolation. A book requires a writer with understanding friends and colleagues. I would like to take this page to thank them for their help, patience, criticism, and most of all, for being there: Joanne Robinson, who I am convinced is the fastest and most accurate typist in Canada; Mairead Stack, who gave me the energy to revise each draft; Jun and Mieke Bevelander, who shared part of their lives with me; and Carole Saltz, who led me through a maze of red-penciled pages.

I would also like to express my deep appreciation to Marshall Hamilton and Jakob Amstutz for their thoughtful contributions both on and off paper; to Steve Fleming, who contributed the section on "Childhood Bereavement" in Chapter 5 while he co-edited *Essence;* and to my students.

Introduction

The fear of death is indeed the pretense of wisdom, and not real wisdom, for it is a pretense of knowing the unknown; and no one knows whether death, which men in their fear apprehend to be the greatest evil, may not be the greatest good. Is not this ignorance of a disgraceful sort, the ignorance which is the conceit that a man knows what he does not know.

Plato, *The Apology*, 428–347 B.C.

It is the child who holds the secrets . . . to this ancient riddle of death, and of our methods of handling and coping with this fearful eventuality . . . .

C.W.Wahl, 1959, p. 19

Although there has been an increasing number of articles and books dealing with death-related issues, little in the way of published materials has been concerned with children's conceptions of how we die. This is unfortunate, especially in light of the curiosity, problems, and anxieties demonstrated by children's questions about death.

For example, if children of five years or younger perceive death as life under changed circumstances, then it makes sense for them to ask if "dead people eat the same kind of foods as we do."

A major objective of this book is to allow children to share with us what they know of death. This is a very important consideration, since most child development texts "have said little about the possible effects of death thoughts and experiences upon the total developmental pattern. The implication has been that this is not an important topic" (Kastenbaum, 1977, p. 115).

The book describes and criticizes some of the studies dealing with the socio-cultural and cognitive development of children. It features the drawings of death provided by 201 Canadian children ranging in age from 3.5 to 12.5 years.

I have asked Dr. Jakob Amstutz, a former student of Piaget and friend of Jung, to write one of the prefaces to the book; and have asked Dr. Marshall Hamilton, a developmental psychologist who is now directing a community-based program for the elderly in southern California, to write another. These choices reflect the fact that the areas to be explored are a blend of philosophical and psychological positions.

The first chapter provides some necessary background information with respect to the child's first experiences with death, the influences on the development of his conceptions about death, and the child's relationship to death from a historical perspective. Chapters 2 through 4 are divided into age groupings, and examine the physiological, social, and cognitive-emotional development of the child within these groupings, with particular emphasis on the development of death conceptions. Selected drawings of death will be included, along with analyses of their contents. Chapter 5 summarizes and integrates the child's changing pattern of beliefs about death; it concludes with a review of the effects of childhood experience with death and bereavement, as well as the problem of talking with children about death.

The reader is to be cautioned that, although the chapter headings reflect a chronological progression, children's conceptions about death seem to develop as do their conceptions in other areas. They begin with an apparent lack of any concept, move gradually to incomplete understanding, and then on to adultlike comprehension. The development of children's conceptions of death is part of their total cognitive development and is not simply a function of their age. The chronological approach taken in this book is intended to serve as a guide rather than as a set of unbending rules for such development, for the relationship between cognitive and chronological development is yet to be defined precisely.

> . . . We have to know what constitutes a well developed orientation toward death. . . . But it is questionable that either our learned disciplines or our society in general possess a single, well documented framework for determining what constitutes the most mature orientation toward death. Despite this limitation, it will be important to follow the continual pattern of death orientations from early childhood onward. . . . The study of the child's relationship with death from the first glimmer of mortality onward can provide useful information for all those who have children in their lives.
>
> Kastenbaum, 1977, pp. 116–117

1

An Orientation

> ¸Death is very much a part of the fantasy thoughts of children. It is also a part of a child's everyday life—the games he plays, the stories he hears, the books he reads, the television programmes he watches, the movies he sees. . . .
>
> Bluebond-Langner, 1974, p. 171

> . . . little people like to look at dead birds, kick dead animals, talk of soldiers or grannies who died . . . . Eventually they even learn that pork chops come from dead pigs.
>
> Kavanaugh, 1972, pp. 127–128

Early Experience

It has been suggested that at the approach of death, the separation between the inner world and that of the world outside becomes more and more diffuse (Kavanaugh, 1972; Kübler-Ross, 1969). As adults, we might see this as a confusion of, or a failure to distinguish between, subjective and objective realities, as well as a sign of cognitive immaturity. We have accused certain groups of holding such views, including artists, writers, musicians, certain physical and social scientists, persons holding various psychopathological titles, and children. As children, we ourselves were so accused by adults. However, if the fusion of the subjective and objective is a reasonably accurate portrayal of the young child's perception of the world (Piaget, for one, has noted that this perceptual state is descriptive of very young children), then the child has had an experience with death. This experience is closer to death and is more dramatic, fascinating, and perhaps fearful than any that we, as adults, can recall. Forgotten though they may be, we did have such experiences!

In spite of our experiences with death, and the child's historical relation to death (pp. 11–17), we remain uncertain and confused about discussing death with our children. We even try to avoid situations in which children can tell us what they know of death."

Reports of first experiences with death generally have been about the death of an animal, and the performance of a sacred rite to ensure the safe passage of the animal to another place. Kavanaugh (1972) has pointed out that "stamping on ants on the sidewalk" was probably his first experience, and suggested that this event was repeated without great psychic damage to him. Even Darwin has reported his killing of worms, again without later detrimental effects. In contrast, Kastenbaum (1977) has suggested that even such "apparently trivial experiences as [the death of a] caterpillar and [a] blossom" can have pronounced effects on personality development.

Anthony (1973) has suggested further that children identify unconsciously with a small animal. This position has been extended and stated with more flair and brilliance by Kafka. Nonetheless, the relationship between children and animals seems an odd combination of mutual acceptance and power.

Maurer (1966) has argued that the earliest relationship the child has with death is a result of the infant's awareness of periodic patterns of sleeping and waking, which establishes the basis for the child to develop perceptions of different states of existence:—

"being" and "nonbeing." This position attempts to trace the child's reported association of sleep with death and to link it to a later awareness of the possibility of the death of the self, which comes once the child has developed an ego structure.

One thing is clear from reports of children's first experiences with death, and that is that such first awareness does not always lead to sadness. There is, of course, a great sadness surrounding the first experience when it is the child who is dying (Easson, 1970; Debuskey, 1970; Furman, 1964(b); Howell, 1967; Knudson and Natterson, 1960; Futterman and Hoffman, 1970). However, Spinetta (1974) points out that one also must be aware of the differences between the anxieties and concerns felt by the parents, as opposed to those felt by the fatally ill child; that parents, physicians, and nurses all must recognize their personal difficulties, but this must not allow them the luxury of not dealing with the child's real concerns.

Wahl (1959) has stated that most adults seem to feel that children cannot comprehend death in any form and, therefore, do not need reassuring. Wahl's work suggests that we are more comfortable with the assumption that children are too young to be concerned about death, and so we do not want to challenge it. Our beliefs in what children know about sexuality have changed, and it appears that we also will amend our beliefs as to what they know about life and death.

There is some concern and anxiety about the later negative effects of early death-related experiences. At present, there is not enough evidence to support the notion of early experiences leading to abnormalities in functioning in later life; however, the evidence that does exist seems to focus on the occurrence and intensity of later depressive states (see Chapter 5). Templer (1976) has recently commented on the nature of the links between death, anxiety, and depression. Added to this discussion are the effects of mourning on children at varying ages. The mourning process has been examined in relation to the death of a brother or sister (Rosenblatt, 1967) and of parents (McConville et al., 1970), and its influence on emotional development. The results of such studies 1) have indicated that patterns of mourning are a function of age and developmental level, 2) have demonstrated some of the adaptations children make to traumatic events, and 3) have shown that mourning behaviors are determined by a complex of internal (intrapsychic) and external (the forms of social interaction) factors (Bowlby, 1969; Sharl, 1961).

Children's Conceptions: Some Suspected Sources of Influence

As children's concepts of death develop, they tend towards those of the society in which they are raised and will probably spend their later years. Recognition of this tendency to conform to societal conceptions has resulted in the growing literature on the effects of violence in the media (Gerbner, 1972; Larson, Gray, and Fortis, 1968; Singer, 1970; Eron et al., 1972; Chaffee and McLeod, 1972; Feshback and Singer, 1971). These studies have implied that television is replacing the family as the teacher of life and its crises; in particular, they have accused the animated cartoon of being the teacher of assaultive behaviors. Cartoons also teach the child about rebirth, and this is a point badly omitted. Reviews of the studies of media effects have found that, whatever the results, they are at best inconsistent, and that more research is needed. Some indirect evidence of media effects has been noted by the following:

1. There is less use of visually-oriented personification symbols of death by North American children than by European children. This is not easily explainable in that television is a visual medium.
2. Koocher (1973) concluded that the effects of the media may be more a function of specific subcultural influences (for example the midwestern value placed upon a matter-of-fact and detailed approach to problems) than of the content of television programs.

On a larger scale, Safier (1964) has commented on the cultural differences influencing cognitive development for Piaget's Swiss children of the 1920s, Nagy's children of the 1940s, and contemporary children.

Although a good deal of effort has gone into the scientific study of media effects on children, there has not been a corresponding attempt to examine the influence of literature on children. Baring-Gould and Baring-Gould (1962) did note that in 1937 Professor Allen Abbot urged nusery rhyme reform, as did Geoffrey Hall in 1949. In their report on Handley-Taylor's analysis of nursery rhymes, it is noted that about 100 out of 200 traditional rhymes deal with the glories and beauty of life, but the other 100 deal with the many ways in which humans and animals die or are mistreated. The contents of these latter 100 nursery rhymes describe murders (n = 8), choking to death (n = 2), death by unknown means (n = 27), torment and cruelty (n = 12), maimings (n = 15), misery and sorrow (n = 16), children being lost or abandoned (n = 9), and poverty and want (n = 9). (The other two are by nonspecific means.) It is also reported that expressions of fear, anguish, pain and selfishness could be found in almost every other page of the rhymes.

Schur (1971) examined literature written for young children as a way of clarifying man's historical attitudes towards death. This approach is based upon the assumption that an individual's perception of death might be found in what he tells children of death. The literature was divided into four categories: 1) Anonymous, 2) Puritan, 3) Intermediate, and 4) Contemporary. The Anonymous period is characterized by the ambiguity of definitions about death, such as found in "Old Mother Hubbard." The literature of the Puritan period contained frequent death themes, stressing the Puritan view that the life of earthly man is sinful and that one must first pass through death to achieve salvation. Death awareness was an awesome threat used to shape the "good" behavior of their children. The Intermediate period, according to Schur, simply took less firm stands on the issues of "religion, threat, and didactism" (p. 86) in relation to the earlier

Puritan position, although the influence of religious belief is still apparent.

> There is an hour when I must die,
> Nor do I know how soon 'twill come;
> A thousand children young as I
> Are call'd by death to hear their doom.
>
> Let me improve the hours I have,
> Before the day of grace is fled;
> There's no repentance in the grave,
> Nor pardons offer'd to the dead.
>
> Just as a tree cut down that fell
> To north, or southward, there it lies;
> So Man departs to heaven or hell,
> Fixt in state wherein he dies.

The stories of Hans Christian Anderson and the Brothers Grimm are examples of Contemporary period literature. In these fairy tales, death is a major figure. The Little Match Girl was chosen by Schur to typify this period, as it is a story of life and death—and life again (in this case with God). In this period, "life is seen as a constant struggle against death," and a constant regeneration. Schur also notes that twentieth-century children's literature represents a shift in the role that illustration played. Children who cannot read can become involved in a book of pictures. In general, this literature attends to the details of how one achieves a good life after death. More important, recent literature has reversed the trends found in the nineteenth century, where death themes were relatively more acceptable.

Hall (1965) examined attitudes toward death found in poetry as "a mirror in which man sees himself reflected" (p. 71). He concluded that, although there were a number of expressions of concepts of life and death, a complete picture of death as seen by poets would be

> I desire death yet I fear it. I know it is inevitable. It is like a pale, shadowy, mysterious sleep. It is both mighty and impotent; sometimes it is ennobling. (p. 81)

Religious training has been thought to be a major influence in the development of children's concepts of life and death; however, Anthony (1973) noted that concepts of death were relatively unrelated to religious denominations and, although the belief in an afterlife (in heaven) declined with increasing age of schoolchildren, the belief persisted in each succeeding generation. Work in the area of adult anxieties about death has shown no consistent relationship between religiosity and anxiety (Templer, 1976; Fiefel, 1976).

The Child in History

> . . . less than 75 years ago, death and children were in comradeship, nearly every child had at least one classmate who died.
>
> Kavanaugh, 1972, pp. 125–126

Childhood has been viewed as a "subculture" inhabited by savages, miniature adults, or mythical and magical beings, as noted by Jung and Aries. Children may well be "strangers in a strange land," a land ruled and normed by entities who were once children. In general, childhood is seen in relatively ahistorical terms by the social sciences. Psychologists, in particular, have been guilty of neglecting to learn from the child's *historical* past. This neglect has left wide gaps in our knowledge of children's concepts of life and death.

Death-related experiences are basic to the history of mankind, with changes in attitudes toward death marking periods of historical change. It is, therefore, of great importance to understand the development of death-thought systems, as they can serve as markers for the growth of human values and behavior.

An assumption system used, abused, and rejected at various times by various groups within the social sciences holds that the child's mental development parallels the developmental stages of the human race (that is, Recapitulation Theory). The thought processes of the child can, in this way, provide a link between the contemporary adult and primitive man. In what ways, however, is the child *like* primitive man?

Evidence of similarities lies in the persistent attention man has given to life-death relationships, and in the denial of death. Cassirer (1953) felt that "the conception that man is mortal, by nature and essences, seems to be entirely alien to mythical and primitive religious thought"; and Marcovitz (1973) has stated that this also may be "true for children, as well as for the child which each of us carries within himself." Another specific historical similarity is found in the importance that both primitive man and the child have placed on possession of magical powers (that is, their willing of death). Their belief in these powers invokes feelings of both omnipotence and helplessness, as they believe they can, at will, cause injury or death to another, as well as be the victims of the will of others. Historical shifts in attitudes about life and death also can find a parallel in the development of children's concepts from an external to an internal orientation. Their concepts move from a focus on some outside agent, whether spiritual or physical, who is responsible for death, to concern about the processes of dying.

Further comparisons between children and primitive man have suggested that both are noble and possess innate goodness; other viewpoints have stressed their savage and morally corrupt nature. Are children savages because they express their feelings freely? We do tend to associate this type of behavioral response with primitive man, even in the face of the philosophical proposal that feelings have no morality. They are just feelings, and the idea of a morality-immorality continuum as applied to feelings is inappropriate.

Borkeneau (1955), in his examination of the historical evolution of life and death concerns, described the emergence of burial rites during the middle paleolithic period as suggesting an enlarged awareness of mortality and an uncertainty about the relation of life to death. Rituals of the latter part of this period reflected the earlier denial of death while elaborating ideas of a life after death.

Attitudes further shift toward death defiance rather than death denial. This former position accepts death but attempts to transcend it. Borkeneau concluded that every culture tries to synthesize these two positions but can achieve such a balance for a short time at best, if at all.

The cycle of historical death-related concerns suggests that "civilizations . . . terminate with a concept of death opposed to that [with] which they started" (p.318). This cycle also can characterize the shift in life and death concerns of young children through adolescence and adulthood; it moves from death denial to death terminality. Borkeneau goes on to say that the collapse of higher civilizations is tied to a return to death denial from death defying, and to the onset of the "dark ages," where contradictions between magic and inevitable death remain unresolved. This pattern of change is not individualized but can be found in clusters of civilizations. Psycholanalysts certainly could have much to say about this pattern of culture-wide defensive reactions. Without going into the preferred defense mechanisms chosen by particular cultures, it seems reasonable to conclude that the denial shown by early societies (early childhood), the acceptance of inevitably shown by later ones (late–middle childhood), and the confusion shown by societies in transition (adolescents' search for identity) provides some intriguing lines for exploration into linking the development of the child to the history of the development of man.

Although Anthony (1973, p.43) states that the Recapitulation Theory has been soundly rejected, she also writes that " . . . uncertainties about death and the thought that the dead should be treated with concern which is not perhaps rationally justified, exemplified in . . . ancient ways, have also been observed in the behavior of children."

Perhaps the link we see most often between the child and primitive man is the most transitory. It may be disfigured to the extent that we see the child as being ignorant, like ancient man, of the "facts" known only to contemporary adults. This ignorance, from the adult viewpoint, is then given as an explanation for the child's (and primitive man's) beliefs in the temporal nature of phenomena, in their cycles, and not in their decay and obsolescence.

Here is a story about three students, aged about 20, who went on a trip to the Alps for several days of mountain climbing. One day, they tried to cross a glacier and one of them fell into a deep crevice. One of the other two boys held the rope while he let his companion down into the crevice. When the rescuer reached the bottom, he saw his friend lying dead with his skull fractured. They could not pull up the dead boy so they crossed the crevice to the hut of the Swiss Alpine Club. While eating the dinner they had in their rucksacks, they saw a dwarf crawl out of the crevice, and watched him cross the glacier and walk towards them.

They panicked and ran into the bedroom, where they wrapped themselves in blankets and crawled under the beds to hide. As they had not come down from the mountains the following day, a rescue group came up and found them wrapped in blankets, still in severe shock, and very frightened. They took the students to the hospital to treat them. Because the students could not tell of the fate that had befallen the third member, the doctors and parents felt that the boys had lost their sanity.

Finally, the father of one of them told the story to his friend, C.G. Jung, who replied, "Bring them to me and I will talk with them." They told Jung the strange and frightening story of the dwarf. Then he told them, "Well, you see, for thousands and thousands of years, our ancestors represented the dead as such tiny beings," and he showed them some icons, idols, little images of the dead flying around, and so on. Then he said,

> All these things that our ancestors have drawn for thousands and thousands of years, are their way of representing forms of thinking [through and] about the world which is still within ourselves. In cases of emergency, accidents and catastrophes, we fall back into representing what happens in these terms and that is what has happened to you.

Jung was trying to teach them how to deal with themselves, and they discovered, at an age that is unusual, the deeper layers of the psyche[1] (Amstutz, 1973).

[1] This story has also been told by C.G. Jung to some of his acquaintances. He also refers to it in *Symbolik Des Geistes*, (Zurich: Rascher Verlag, 1958), p. 25.

Another example of such symbolic representations came to me from a woman in my Psychology of Aging, Dying, and Death class who had a problem that was obviously causing her a good deal of agitation. It seems that her mother was dying and one day she brought her young daughter (aged seven) along while she visited. Her daughter approached her grandmother's bed and proceeded to tell her grandmother that she looked like a bird. The grandmother appeared to be very interested in receiving a full account of just how she was becoming a bird, and touched her face to outline the path of the birdlike changes. The mother was standing nearby throughout this exchange and was terribly upset about her daughter's improprieties. When she told me of this situation, I discussed with her the notion of the bird being a historically important symbol of the transition from this earthly life to another, and suggested that her daughter was in touch with such historical forces, and that, rather than being upset, she should be pleased that her daughter was so sensitive to these forces. She listened, discussed, and remained at least a little confused but less disturbed. A few days later, the woman's mother had a similar conversation with her, adding that she felt that she was indeed becoming a bird and was looking forward to her complete metamorphosis so she could go on to a new life.

Although modern man has tried to shield children from death, children historically have been subjected to death. They have been sacrificed to seal treaties of peace, tortured, burned, murdered, worked to death, and so on. Through a litany of horrors the child finds his place in the recorded history of man. First-born children usually have been in the greatest danger of being murdered and then eaten. Of more recent interest is Schachter's work on sibling position, which has focused upon differences between the first- and later-born child. Perhaps he, too, is tapping into the forces surrounding the growth of man, albeit in a limited way.

The Old Testament presents a series of episodes depicting the relationship between fathers and their children culminating in the relationship between God and His children. Take the example in

Genesis, chapter 22, describing the sacrificing of Isaac by Abra-
ham. However, in the relatively brief history of child development studies, the father has been a rather neglected figure, particularly in studies dealing with the separation anxieties of young
children. The care of the child is only half of the story; the references to the killing of children are many. Freud also has stressed
the killing of the father in discussing the basis of religion. Perhaps
the most notable aspects of the relationship between fathers and
their children are found in the allusions in the Old Testament to
the killing of the child whose paternity was in doubt; or to the
desire to kill the child when the mobility of the family was restricted or food was in short supply; and to the threats of God, as
translated by man, for disobedience.

Bakan (1966) has indicated that the "child in history" is a re-
minder of the physical and spiritual fusion of male and female.
The killing of a child then represents a resistance to this unity. He
further points out that it now is possible to care for and educate
children to an extent that was not possible in earlier stages of the
history of human evolution.

When in widely separated cultures there is a similarity of
development of cognitions and behaviors based upon these
cognitions, we can infer that there is a general propensity for
such behaviors. This line of thought allows us to believe that as
children develop, they will eliminate those constructs that are
not socially acceptable. It is a pattern which seems to promote a
shift from universal truths to those which are attached to speci-
fied cultural values. The development of children's death-related
concepts surely falls prey to such cultural expectations and
manipulations.

We take delight in the difference between ourselves and our
children. Unfortunately, this delight does not extend itself well
when differences are found between our death-related concepts
and those of children. We take joy in our knowledge that children
are capable of perceiving and being influenced by phenomena
differently from adults, and at the same time we are concerned
about the impact this influence has on their fragile innocence. We

also should be concerned about what we can learn from our children and they from us.

> . . . Healthy children will not fear life if their parents have integrity not to fear death.
>
> Erickson, 1950, p. 233

2

The Child from Three through Five Years

Studies of human lifespan development have stressed that at birth the child has a ready-made capability for learning. Invariably, the learning is tied to the adaptations made by the infant to particular feeding schedules. It is remarkable that the drama of coming into the world is not written about as much as the eating patterns that follow. In our lifespan, do we ever again go through such awesome changes? If we, as adults, could recall these events, does it seem likely that we would, after emerging into a world of different rhythms of darkness and light, be so concerned about eating? We are incredibly adaptive organisms, at least during the earlier periods of our lives.

Infancy is marked, as is birth, by a series of events of unimagined importance. Not long after the infant has adjusted to his new surroundings, he has begun the tasks of 1) learning to cope with solid foods, 2) walking and using fine muscles, 3) gaining some control over the processes of differentiation, 4) building the foundation for social speech and communication, 5) achieving some degree of sensory-motor coordination, and 6) in general, learning to relate to other life forms in his environment. What does our adult world have to match the triumph of a three year old who can ride a tricycle, when we consider that at four weeks the child could not support the weight of his head unaided and, at forty weeks, he was just mastering sitting and crawling? Moreover, consider the magnitude of the cognitive-motor jump from just being able to make brief eye movements to follow an object at four weeks of age, to being able to use the thumb and index finger for the manipulation of toys at forty weeks, to drawing "houses" at three years of age.

Developmental Concerns

The child of three to five years of age has been examined in relation to how he is approaching, in terms of his physical and socio-emotional development, the status of "miniature adult." First, during this period, the child develops the ability to communicate with others and learns to understand what others are communicating to him. Second, he refines the concepts of social and physical realities in culturally directed ways. Third, he learns the appropriate ways in which to relate emotionally with others, particularly with his parents; and fourth, he comes to terms with the social values that will influence later development. During this period of growth, one also can see parents express their desire for their child to be unique, yet not so unique that he will be considered to be abnormal when compared behaviorally and intellectually to other children of a similar age.

The study of how children develop the facility to deal with abstractions and culturally derived symbols has attracted a number of researchers (examples are Piaget, 1960; Penfield and Roberts, 1958; Hebb, 1949). This work has suggested quite strongly that the pattern of perceptual-motor development during the first six or seven years of life is crucial for later successful adaptations to life. The first two years of development are directed at strengthening simple motor responses. The next three years focus upon the development of language and the use of symbols to represent objects in the world, along with the development of a visual awareness of the world that implies the increased emphasis upon the symbolic associations of such perceptions. The period of middle childhood (about eight years of age) through adolescence is largely concerned with cognitive development; that is, the integration of sensory imputs and concepts about the world, coupled with the search for personal identity.

The shift most often noted in the development of language usage is the asking of "why" (about the age of four) rather than "what" (about the age of two). This shift appears to be a marker of the child's growing interest in trying to understand how things operate in his world. There is a corresponding shift in the size of the child's average vocabulary, from about 900 words at age three to more than 2000 words at age five (Lenneberg, 1964), and in the child's ability to present his views of the world to others by drawing what he sees. Along with these changes, there is the psychosocial crisis of initiative versus guilt (Erikson, 1950). This features the fulfillment of the child's needs for direction and purpose, centering around how his parents perceive his actions along these lines; for example, playing versus making things.

Another change in the use of language by the child of four to seven years of age is the more frequent use of the word "because." The reason this word has achieved such importance is due to its observed relationship to the degree of egocentricism of the child and his notion of cause and effect. The symbolic contents of language now serve to associate ideas with one another and help to remove the child from the center of his perceptual universe, replacing the immensely important centralized self with a more socially acceptable self, one who can communicate with, influence, and be influenced by, others. The child, at this level of development, still cannot deal effectively with concepts of time, space, measurement, and movement (Piaget, 1954). Instead, he attends to one aspect of each situation or event, for he is certain that things are as they appear to be. Such preoperational thought is said to be animistic in nature, as movement becomes associated with consciousness and the quality of being alive. When the child becomes more familiar with imposed cause-and-effect relationships, less egocentric, and more initiating, he will tend to mediate his views of the world by using the terms "since" and "because." Language becomes a filter for his curiosity about the world, on both the input and output side, for he not only will ask different questions about the nature of events (*why* versus *what*), but will also encode the answers he receives, using his newly found and growing ability to manipulate verbal representations of the events he is interested in. Piaget has stated that this world does not begin until after two years of age, or when the child has developed the "words" for such representations.

Time-related and number concepts are felt to exist only as vague shadows for the child of three to five years of age (Cohen, Hansel, and Sylvester, 1954; Wohlwill and Wiener, 1964). Before the age of six or seven, the child has great difficulty telling time by using a clock; and he has not developed ideas about the duration of days, months, or years. The child has a fluid notion of time, as there is little perceived difference between these time designations. Time is bound to feelings of hunger (for some children time can be measured by the number of sandwiches that can be eaten in an hour), or tiredness, or of wanting to play. At about four or five years of age, children can distinguish the days of the week, but which month or year it is has not yet become meaningful.

Children ask questions that hold meaning for them, and some of their questions concern life and death (Anthony, 1973; Kavanaugh, 1972; Kastenbaum and Aisenberg, 1972; Natterson and Knudson, 1960). The birth concepts expressed by young children are magical rather than biological. Is not birth an event of this status? Even biologists would concur that the birth of a human being can be thought of as "an improbable event." Whorf (1956), in his classic work with the Hopi, reported that as their language system lacked symbols to represent causal relationships, they conceived of birth as a spiritual event.

It is important to realize that language development is associated not only with increasing refinements of social skills, but also with nonphysical approaches to problem solving. Words are remembered, used to make generalizations, applied to new situations the child encounters, and their increased usage tends to be perceived by parents as a signal both of new frustrations to deal with, and of the child's growing awareness of the world. The child's social world, however, is still enclosed by his immediate surroundings, which includes his play activities. At the age of three, play begins to take on the aspects of the theater. There is a noticeable increase in combining toys and playmates in imaginative ways; this further increases in the next year as children's play becomes more complicated and dramatic. At the age of five, these earlier features of play are retained and add to the building of friendships and to the balancing of competitiveness with cooperativeness. Play can serve to help children cope with their fears, whether real, imaginary, or anticipated; and children at the age of five are good at playing. Such activities also provide the child with the channels to develop his emerging social self, since he now can make decisions, perceive the consequences, and perhaps try it another way the next time he goes out to play. The child can experiment with the types of social roles that he may find useful in later stages of development. Play allows him to try out a series of value judgments that will help him to create a comfortably fitting self-image. The child is undergoing and participating in a social upheaval. In this development of an image to present to the world, the child may copy what he sees others do. We do not want our children to appear weak or be afraid, so we strive not to show this side of us to them for fear they may copy behaviors based on what we feel to be an inappropriate model. We emphasize the brave but not the gentle, the courageous but not the humane. It is an artificial view of the world that can cause the child a good deal of confusion, especially when issues of life and death are in question.

An example of our bias in the study of young children can be seen in the abundant literature devoted to the effects of the "new baby" on the socio-emotional development of the other children in the family, as compared to the virtual absence in the literature on the effects of the "loss of siblings" on such development.

The average five year old weighs about 41 pounds, with males being slightly heavier than females, and are about 43 inches tall (Gardner, 1969; Watson and Lowrey, 1958). The child at this age seems to take life as it comes. He plays about 75% of the time, and is affectionate toward his parents, especially toward his mother (Skonsen, 1962). How can one interfere with the activities of this delightful little creature by discussing how we die? The child of five does have ideas about life and death, and is interested in talking about these ideas.

Conceptual Considerations: Animism, Causality and Separation, and Time

> . . . Because of this seeming ability to look now at the present, now at the past, now at the future, the sensation of there being a constant thinker separate from the flow of events is all the more plausible.
>
> Watts, 1973, pp.163–164

The development of concepts of animism, causality and separation, and time has been explored from a variety of philosophical and psychological perspectives and has been thought of as associated with the child's development of ideas about life and death. At least a brief introduction to those concepts is therefore a necessary step toward detailed discussions of children's death-related concerns.

The child can represent a sort of fragile tunnel whereby the past can find its way into the present, even if at times the child appears to be inconsistent and absurd. At first the infant is fascinated to find himself transported out of one existence into another. He is full of energy that can take the form of unending cries and screams, of reaching out and feeling, and of exploring the nature of the solidarity of objects in his world. A little later, this infant may awake in the night and find himself alone. He may now want food and water near his bed and the light to be left on when he sleeps. He may act as if he saw his reflection for the first time, became entranced by it, and soon forgot that it was merely a reflection and began treating this created self as real being [see Watt's (1964) discussion of the creation of the "God-head"]. This process of change can be seen in the development of social language, in which the richly and clearly known qualities of inner language of early childhood are overcome by a learned system of communication. This takeover would not be so terrible if both language systems could exist; unfortunately, the artificial one dominates and the inner one recedes (Vygotsky, 1962). Conceptualizations will shift from an earlier period of mysticism to one of biological imperatives and then onward to a system of social determinism (Vernon and Payne, 1973).

Animism

Controversies still rage over the interpretations placed upon animism in children (Piaget, 1952a,b; Tallmer, Fornanck, and Tallmer, 1974; Safier, 1964); however, the point remains that ideas about what is alive and what is dead are related. The word itself has alluded to a system of philosophical or religious beliefs, as well as to a basis for physical laws. The animism of the child, according to Piaget (1960), falls into four stages. In each successive stage, there is decreasing use of animistic explanations for behaviors.

1. The stage at which will is attributed to inanimate objects. In this way, if we explore the humor of Woody Allen, with respect to his routines devoted to attacks on his person engineered by chairs, lights, tables, rugs, and so on, we might see his humor in a different way.
2. The stage at which will is attributed to everything that moves; this seems to occur at about the age of seven or eight years.
3. The stage at which will is attributed to things that apparently move by themselves; this occurs beyond eight years of age.

4. The stage at which will is attributed to things in much the same way as adults attribute such characteristics.

These stages are not so clearly defined as the list may imply. In fact, many problems of a predominantly semantic nature remain in terms of what is life, living, animate, or inanimate—for children ascribe "living" to objects that are not described as being animals, such as trees. Tallmer, Fornanck, and Tallmer (1974) have reported that distinctions between animate and inanimate forms seem to appear before the child can express adultlike concepts of death.

Safier (1964) found, in studies of boys four to ten years of age, a three-stage developmental progression of animism and death-related concerns that tended to support the work of Nagy (1948) and Piaget (1960).

1. The youngest of children saw life and death in terms of constant flux and interchange.
2. Children in the middle of this age range saw life and death given and taken away by an outside agent.
3. The older children saw life and death as part of an internal principle which indicated that when something wants to stop, it will.

A most interesting point to consider is that the child's view of the world does not differ from that of the adult in terms of immaturity and ignorance, but does differ in terms of the child's acceptance and tolerance of ambiguities. It is of some value to note that it is this very tolerance for variant views that we attribute to artistic and scientific creativity, and even genius.

The findings with respect to children's animistic concepts seem to differ as a function of the views of the investigator (Jahoda, 1958; Huang and Lee, 1945; Piaget, 1952 a,b); yet the same findings form a consensus of opinion about the idea that below the conscious level the conceptualizations of adults may well be animistic.

In summary, animism has been related to

1. The general development of children across different cultures
2. Differences within cultures.

In the first case, the assumption has been that initially there is little or no differentiation between subjective and objective realities or between the self and the world of objects. Within the boundaries of this view, the self is animate. The inanimate classification appears before the use of social language, and has been seen as being related to the handling and movement of objects. The role animism plays in a specific culture is assumed under number 2. Childhood education, as it relates to concepts of animism, will be determined by the values the culture places on such views, basically in terms of survival. If concepts of animism can lead to danger, then such views will be extinguished early. Concepts of life and death are a function of discovery, experimentation, and language; they may not be interpreted so simply as saying that what does not move by itself is not alive.

Causality and Separation

The development of concepts of causality and separation has been seen to be a crucial phase in intellectual development. These concepts are thought to have a major influence on emotional development as well (Anthony, 1973; Erikson, 1950). Specifically, the onset of causal notions is heralded by a shift in children asking "why" rather than "what" questions. "Why" questions are unnecessary at an earlier stage of development, because it is the stage at which the subjective and objective are fused into a unitary view of the world that includes the very young observer himself. Questions of motives and causes achieve importance only when a separation is perceived between the subjective and objective.

"Why" questions can arise out of the child's fascination with the immediately experienced world, especially when such fascination is attached to the occurrence of new or unexpected events.

The first "why" question may be one of surprise at the perception and/or experience of events of this type. Although these events start out as unexpected, they soon can appear with some regularity. It is the perception of the occurrence of a series of initially unexpected events that can trigger another set of perceptions of separation from, or loss of control over the delicate balance of, the fused subjective-objective world. Perceptions of separation or loss of control can lead to feelings in the child of the presence of other forces in the world, which are powerful and not understood and can "cause" things to happen. These forces pry the child away from his unitary views, and separate him from a part of his earlier world. Death now comes to mean separation, disappearance, and loss (Nagy, 1948; Anthony, 1973). Piaget has written that all seems well to the child until awareness of life and death differences initiates a search for causal explanations. This search is accompanied by a growing elaboration of socially approved rules and rituals for coping with the emergence of other-world views.

The search for causality may be seen as a way of coping with the separation of the subjective from the objective. It is a search for the ties that hold the subjective self to the objective world. Causality implies a reaching back for that self as an elemental part of an earlier view of the world. This search carries with it a need to examine the nature of the association between time and the phenomena of the objective world. What the child is searching for, along with the "laws of causal association," are ways of coping with separation. Adults who observe the games children play note that fantasy and reincarnation seem to be the ways of achieving mastery over feared experiences. As an example, Maurer's (1966) analysis of the game peek-a-boo ("alive or dead") includes the suggestion that the child is attempting to gain mastery over the coming and going phenomena, that of disappearing temporarily (being dead) and reappearing again at another time (being alive). The games of cowboys and Indians and cops and robbers are full of conversations about who is dead after they have been shot by a fierce cap pistol or a finger. When we were growing up, we solved this problem quite easily by using water guns. If you were wet, you were dead, which goes against earlier ideas that children associate wetness with life and dryness with death. At the time, however, we were more concerned about the application of the rules of the game and penalties for not obeying them.

Observation of children at play does provide information about their life and death concerns, not just on a limited time scale, but on a historical one, for the rituals of games have existed for centuries.

Another way of coping with the growing feelings of separateness is to develop concepts related to the interchangeability of life forms and objects. Kastenbaum (1977, p. 129), in his discussion of children's first experiences with death, stated that a dead groundhog may not stimulate anxiety or interest about mortality, as there is a seemingly endless supply of lookalikes running around. There are a number of questions a child can raise concerning the transfer of the "replacement theory" to people, however, especially to those people of importance to him. If the notion of replacing things extends to the child himself, what then? Because he cannot remember his coming into this life (at least we believe this to be the case), he may come to think of himself as an immediate replacement. Ideas about interchangeability can be an additional source of anxiety about separation, not only from his former world view, but from his present self and his possible past selves. These ideas, set in motion by a new awareness of the relationship between causality and life and death, also can be the beginnings of a worthwhile philosophical view of the self in the world.

Time

The understanding of the relationship between time and death is said to occur in a period before formal socialized education and should be interpreted in this way. The roots of this relationship are traced to our own beginnings in the world, thus they are relatively culture-free and make themselves known through our perception of the appearance and disappearance of objects and people, as well as in the changes in the seasons. In early childhood, there is a confusion, based upon adult norms, of time and being. There is a seeming inability to conceive of time as separate from one's existence; to accept the occurrence of events when one was not there to witness them. This inability, however, is not only restricted to children.

The very young child appears to be devoid of a sense of social history, that is, one that provides a conceptual linkage, in terms of linear time, between age and death. In view of this "conceptual flaw" in the child, he can be said to be external (free of culture), for he believes in cycles of lives and deaths, and has no sense of history or of the irreversibility of change. This flaw is corrected as the child develops language facilities and gradually exchanges his cyclical views for linear ones, his notions of rebirth for those of terminality, and a feeling of cosmic unity for one of immortality.

Every action we take alters the environment which contains our selves; there is change everywhere. We can come to fear such changes and become more comfortable with ideas of patterned regularities and imposed predictabilities. We can become disturbed if we feel we are losing a grasp on these assessments. Such disturbance is exemplified by the desire to make up for lost time or by great concern over how short life really is (Lonetto, Fleming, and Mercer, 1979).

In Western culture, notions of death of the self have become related to and are seen as a consequence of the passage of time and a consequence of growing older, for old age is seen as a preliminary to death. Hall (1965) has indicated that, although life is viewed in poetic terms in both positive and negative ways, it is generally characterized by its short duration.

Research has not drawn any firmly supported conclusions about the exact age or developmental level at which the child understands adult ideas about time, except to say that basic time concepts seem to appear in the period extending from late childhood into early adolescence. Even less work has been done on how the child is affected when his awareness of socially objectified time supercedes his earlier, more phenomenologically oriented, time concepts.

Studies employing measures of time perspectives over the projected lifespan have shown that the latter half of the lifespan was less eventful than the earlier phase and that, in the geriatric years, almost no events of any importance were perceived to occur (Lonetto, 1978; Kastenbaum, 1961).

In view of the limited number of studies relating concepts of time to those of death, perhaps the best statement that can be made is that time has an elasticity that can push one away or pull one toward the fear of death. Supportive evidence for this assumption lies in the reports of a number of investigators who asked subjects to predict their lifespans. The results demonstrated that many people believe they will live longer than they want to, or else they see themselves dying before their life loses its earlier valued qualities, that is, dying at about 54 to 59 years old, a reasonably young age (Kastenbaum and Aisenberg, 1972; Lonetto et al., 1975).

The very young child is not in command of the social language of adults, and is not experienced in expressing himself in their symbol combinations. He may not even be sure that adults share his world view. Through the channels of socialization, the child's perceptions of realities are fitted into the context of his culture. This shifting of world views is accepted as a rite of passage; however, this acceptance does not mean that the child or the adult is no longer confused about life and death.

Children's Concepts of Death: Ages Three through Five

There is hardly what one could call widespread agreement as to the precise age at which the child understands the passage of time and death; however, there is an almost overwhelming feeling that this understanding emerges in the period extending from late childhood into early adolescence. Coexisting with this feeling is the view that the young child cannot conceive of futurity and death in adult terms.

Those areas of the social sciences concerned with the child's development have traditionally maintained that the child of five years of age and younger has *no* understanding of time and death, although research efforts along these lines have been minimal. Even Piaget's determined studies of the developing child leave a good deal unsaid about these concepts. Developmentally oriented researchers have stressed that the adolescent period is the proper time for these concepts to make their full presence known, along with the child's continuing search for identity. It is as if, prior to adolescence, the child is free of such crises but pays for this early innocence in his adolescence, which has been described as a testing period for the future, especially in terms of learning to cope with anxieties related to the self.

Our conceptual links to death are thought to be rooted in birth through the factors of 1) separation, 2) sleep, and 3) the feelings of attachment to earth and water, and of returning to a place both shadowy and safe. Rank (1958) has noted that the birth trauma is paradoxical: on the one hand, it involved a separation from the mother; on the other, a rebirth. Out of these drive states is forged the individualized and cosmic view of the self in time and space.

Throughout the span of life, each new separation reawakens the trauma of birth. It is a feeling that in each separation there are elements of death. In this way, it is from our birth that our anxieties and fear of death are derived. Birth may well be the first separation. For the child, then, cannot death be conceived of as the first unity, a symbolic union of the cycles of life and death and life? Rank (1958) has further commented on this position by pointing out the interchangeability of symbols of life and death found in a number of primitive societies.

The very young child is perceived to be the most vulnerable to, and the most disturbed by, any type of separation. It is well worth bearing in mind, however, that our understanding of the attitudes and behaviors of children has been influenced by the passage of time (Aries, 1962; Wolfenstein, 1951). That is, children may have developed only to the extent that our perceptions of such development allow, and in accordance with our views of their place in society. Whatever the range of changing expectations and views of children, we seem to be bewildered most of the time by our children. It has been suggested that this bewildered state is translated into the treatment of children by adults, which, as Fontana (1964) states, can range from abuse to neglect and can be classified as a maltreatment syndrome.

Studies of Children's Concepts of Death

Maria Nagy. This researcher's work on "the child's theories" concerning death appeared in the *Journal of Genetic Psychology* in 1948. Of interest is that, in her introduction, Nagy recognized that the child's conceptions of death were still "isolated" from the general area of developmental studies, and that research was needed to investigate the theories on the nature of death held by a child of from three to ten years of age. This state of affairs still exists.

Nagy collected information from children aged three through ten, in three ways: 1) the six-to-ten year olds were each asked to write about "everything that comes into your mind about death"; 2) in addition to their compositions, the six-to-ten year olds were asked to provide drawings; 3) discussions were held with both the three-to-six year olds and the seven-to-ten year olds in which each child was asked, basically, to "tell me all you can think of about death." When the child's repertoire of responses appeared to be exhausted, Nagy posed the following questions:

1. What is death?
2. Why do people die?
3. How do you recognize when someone is dead?
4. Do you usually dream? Tell me what you dream about.

With the three-to-six year olds, Nagy reported having a somewhat more difficult time with these discussions, as compositions were not completed by each child upon which to base discussion.

She would try first to establish contact with the child and ask him to tell her about something in the room, and then proceed to ask about such words as birth, life, death, and brother. Her follow-up questions were similar to those listed above. Of the 378 Hungarian children tested in and around Budapest, 51% were boys, 49% were girls, and 39 children were from three to five years of age.

The results of this research have been grouped into three stages of development of death-related concepts for children of from three to ten years of age.

Stage 1. Children under five years of age did not see death as irreversible but rather as a living on under changed circumstances. Eighty-six percent of the three year olds, 50% of the four year olds, and 33% of the five year olds were at this level of conceptual development.

Stage 2. Children between the ages of five and nine years personified death. Fourteen percent of the three year olds, 50% of the four year olds, and 67% of the five year olds were found to be at this level of conceptual development.

Stage 3. Children beyond nine years of age saw death as final and lawful. No child five years of age or younger was classified at this conceptual level.

The first stage of development, for the child five years of age and under, is marked by attributing life processes and consciousness to the dead. Two other dominant themes of this age range are the association of death with sleep (this view has been examined in light of the child's denial of death), and the association of death with life (that is, death is seen as a gradual or temporary state).

A boy of five-and-one-half years said to his friend of the same age: " . . . they bury them [the dead] in the earth and tell you they [the dead] are in heaven."
His friend replied: "Oh you know, they have tunnels"

Amstutz, 1978

Death to these children is a departure, a living on in some other place. The most influential aspect of this conception is that of separation. If anyone goes away from the child, they may be considered to be dead. A person doesn't simply disappear, he must live somewhere! Children at this stage of development often ask questions concerning just where the person went and how they are getting on. The dead can live on in the cemetery, although under conditions of restricted mobility. Some questions may be asked about why caskets are not buried vertically rather than horizontally, as the dead should be able to speak to each other and see each other, and about how the dead can get proper nourishment.

Life and death can change places with one another. The dead are living in another place, waiting to return. Children five years of age and under are expressing their notion of rebirth, of the cycles and changes in the ways of existence. This stage of development is best summarized by children attributing life to everything. There is no such thing as lifelessness. It is a stage at which animism encloses death.

Notions of aging are not reported, while time-related concerns can be seen to be associated with the disappearance-emergence cycles of significant others in the child's life, and with the cycles of wakefulness-sleepfulness.

Sylvia Anthony. In her much quoted work (1973) on the relationship between death concepts and the age of the child, she explored children's discovery of death in three ways:

1. By using parental records, either from her specific research or that published by other researchers
2. By inserting children's definitions of the word 'dead' into the vocabulary scale of the Terman-Merrill form of the Binet scale
3. By giving children a story completion exercise.

Her subjects for this 1940 study consisted of 128 children (71 boys and 57 girls) from different areas in and around the city of

London, England, who ranged in age from under 5 years to 13 years, 11 months. The attempt to relate death concepts to the age of the child involved classifying the responses of the children into five categories. These categories were reported to be relatively free of religiosity.

A. Apparent ignorance, by adult standards, of the meaning of the word "dead"
B. Interest in word or fact, combined with limited or erroneous concept
C. No evidence of noncomprehension of the meaning of "dead," but definition given by reference to a) associated phenomena not biologically or logically essential, or b) humanity specifically
D. Correct, essential, but limited reference
E. General, logical, or biological definition or description

Anthony reported that no child under the age of five gave responses that fit in the C category; that is, they all fell into the A and B categories. No child under eight years of age responded in the D or E category. These findings lead to the conclusion that there is a positive association between age and conceptual development, more so for mental age than chronological age. A crucial point for change in this development occurred between ages seven and eight, as every child gave a response in the C category, which in some part may be due to the effects of schooling.

There were certain categories of responses given by children of from three to five years of age, to the word "dead" and to the story completion exercise. Characteristic responses that fit within the A category indicated a failure, in adult terms, to give definitions of the word "dead."

> (Reported by school teacher) Marlene (2 years, 11 months) was brought to school by her father, who had found her lying asleep beside her dead mother on the floor by a half-made bed. The mother had apparently suffered a heart attack. On arrival at school, Marlene said quite happily to the teacher, "Mother lay down on the floor and went to sleep, so I went to sleep too."

> Ursala (3 years, 4 months), while playing with her mother, found a dead moth in the garden and discovered that it could not move. She said, "Like the crab at St. Leonard's, and there was a boy took the pail and got water and put it in to see if it would move and it didn't move. Why didn't it move, Mummie?"

Anthony also stated that the imitative behaviors of children aged three to five years further serves to demonstrate their lack of comprehension.

B category reponses showed an interest in death, combined with a limited and erroneous set of concepts.

> Phineas (3 years, 9 months) had not before seen the others cut dead animals up, and was puzzled. He had no clear idea of death and asked several times, "Why are you killing it?" The other children laughed and assured him . . . that it was dead. Presently, he said, "Is it dead, nearly?"

A cross-cultural comparison is provided by Anthony in her presentation of Chinese children's views of "life" and "living." One hundred percent of these children under six years of age classified a dog as both living and having the qualities of life; however, only 52.4% of the children thought a tree to be living, and 33.3% attributed the qualities of life to a tree. Another example of the relationship between perceived movement and life and death is found in the following example.

> The rabbit had died in the night. Dan (4 years) found it and said, "It's dead—its tummy doesn't move up and down now." Paul (4 years, 2 months) said, "My daddy says that if we put it into water, it will get alive again." Mrs. I said, "Shall we do so and see?" They put it into a bath of water. Some of them said, "It's alive." Duncan (7 years, 1 month) said, "If it floats, it's dead, and if it sinks, it's alive." It floated . . . . One of them said, "It's alive, because it's moving." This was a circular movement, due to the current in the water. Mrs. I therefore put in a small stick which also moved round and round, and they agreed that the stick was not alive. They then suggested that they should bury the rabbit.

The child of about four years of age, according to Anthony, is confused about the state of a dead animal, as the child tends to see the animal as being asleep, not moving, but capable of movement as soon as it wakes up. Death is then a function of the perceived state of immobility. Kane (1975), in her study of 122 children aged 3 through 12 years of age, also found that the child's concepts of death included immobility, as well as separation.

The development of children's death conceptions was also studied by Anthony through analysis of their fantasies. Children were asked to complete a series of stories, such as

1. "One day the father and mother were annoyed with each other, and they quarrelled, and the reason was . . .?"
2. "One Sunday the boy (or, they all) went out for the day with his (their) father and mother; when they came home in the evening, the mother was very sad. Why?"
3. "The boy had a friend he liked very much; one day his friend came to him and said, 'You come with me and I'll tell you a secret, and show you something, but you mustn't tell anyone about it.' What did he show him? What did he tell him?"
4. "When the girl went to bed at nighttime, what did she think about?"
5. "Then the fairy gave her $100,000 to spend. What did she do with it?"

Some of the death references found in completion of the story openings were:

1. "They wanted to get rid of their children."
2. a. "Because she had lost something—or perhaps somebody died."
   b. "Because she'd lost one of her children." (How?) "The child was paddling in the water, and a great big fish came up and ate her."
   c. "Because the father—because somebody might have died down there, the father or anybody."
3. (Long silence; then speech hurried and indistinct) ". . .

don't mind saying . . . a boy just say . . . that his mother was dead."
4. "About someone would come in her room and kill her."
5. "Save it, and buy something nice—a present for her mother or a bunch of flowers to put on her father's grave."

The grief and distress shown by parents in these stories, especially that shown by the mother, was viewed by children as being attributed to the loss of a child or a separation from the child. When fear was expressed in the story completions, death appeared in a violent and assaultive context, usually externalized in the form of a shadowy or ghostlike figure; however, this latter fantasy production was more common for children above five years of age. Anthony summarized the fantasies of her young subjects as showing that they saw death as "a sorrow-bringing thing and a fear-bringing thing; grievous because it involves separation of child and parent, or of parents from each other; and frightening as the consequence of malevolence in action, either one's own or that of other people."

These fantasies also involved the association of death with sleep, through the cycling of figures who can die and become alive again. Fantasy productions were analyzed as the child's ways of attempting to maintain some sort of control over feared events through the control of mental imagery. Children's play that exhibited their fantasies about 'killing' was also examined; it was thought to be a relatively harmless form of expression that does not lead to later pathological problems.

Play, as noted earlier, represents an additional form of mastery over fear, through fantasy. Anthony felt that children's anxiety about death, in moderation, was not only normal but inevitable, and could explain their use of "magic" as a way of coping with feelings of this kind.

What of children who have had some contact with death situations? The themes of their responses to the story completion exercise were generally of punishment. This finding is somewhat supported and extended by the work of McConville (1970), Brown (1961, 1966), Bowlby (1969, 1973), Moriarity (1967), and Sharl (1961). These studies into the mourning and bereavement patterns of children report that up until the age of about eight years, the child uses regression, denial, hopelessness, and animistic fantasies in order to deal with the sadness of the death of a parent or sibling. Although younger children did seem to want to avoid discussion of specific deaths, some researchers were quite amazed at the adaptations made by children that showed their ability to employ cognitive, affective, and integrative strategies. Others saw their regressive behaviors and use of denial as indicative of impaired or restricted ego defenses (Sharl, 1961); still others suggested that bereavement as early as the age of three years can have implications for later development and behaviors related to life crises.

Anthony presents a record of a child (3 years, 9 months) who had expressed a good deal of anxiety about death, but who had not had an experience of dying or death within her family. This child was quite upset that people changed or grew older, and wanted to ascertain through her questions whether everyone had to die when they became old. An interesting problem arose in trying to answer her questions, in that "being old" for this child might be interpreted as her next birthday or even next week. Concerns about aging were centered about her parents growing older, for, if parents did grow old and die, who would take care of the child?

> Ruth (4 years, 7 months): "Will you die, father?" F: "Yes, but not before I grow old." R: "Will you grow old?" F: "Yes." R: "Shall I grow old, too?" F: "Yes." (Three months later) R: "Every day I'm afraid of dying . . . I wish I might never grow old, for then I'd never die, would I?"

More specifically, this concern is that parents will not die before the child "grows up" and can take care of himself. Beliefs in reincarnation may serve as a defense against this feeling of loss for the child, until the role of reversal is more developed or the child turns into the adult and future parent. Part of this belief system places a good deal of emphasis upon the grandparents, who provide another link for the child in the cycle of life changes.

If we examine the other side of these concerns about aging, the conclusion is that children believe that they cannot die, as death only comes to the old. In fact, some very young children may state that death occurs at the age of about 100 years; before that time death is an impossibility. The classification of the dead can then include the old, with advanced age seen as a necessary and sufficient prerequisite to death. Yet, there is death without finality; it is a period of transition into another life. It has been noted recently that the association between old age and death has been reinforced for children by our increased use of institutionalization procedures for the aged, which have effectively made the aged individual "disappear," and causes the child to believe the elder has died.

Anthony summarized her observations of children's conceptions of death by stressing their linkage to birth traumas and to later anxiety and aggressive impulses. This is hardly surprising, in view of her psychoanalytic orientation. She further states that perceptions and cognitions about death are not amenable to study by straight empirical approaches, because they have a tendency to narrow the breadth of such cognitions. Her work seems to suggest that the child can become psychologically isolated from the parents if they do not listen to what their children have to tell them through words, pictures, and actions.

Other Studies. Hall (1922), Schilder and Wechsler (1934), Caprio (1950), Alexander and Alderstein (1958), Von Hug Hellmuth (1965), Steiner (1965), Portz (1965), Harrison, Davenport, and McDermott (1967), and Childers and Wimmer (1971), using varying methodological procedures, provide further reports on the concept of death in childhood. They all investigated the awareness of death as universal and irrevocable.

Of particular concern is the work of Childers and Wimmer (1971), who studied 75 children (38 girls and 37 boys) aged four to ten years of age, in an attempt to test the hypothesis that the child's awareness of death is independent of age. They used the method of individual discussion, followed by this series of questions:

1. Say whatever comes to your mind about death.
2. Have you seen anything or anyone dead? Tell me about it.
3a. What are some things that living people can do?
3b. Which of these things can dead people do?
3c. Does this mean they can come back to life?
4. Does everybody die?
5. Will everybody die?

Their findings showed no clear-cut relationship between the age of the child, experience, and acceptance of death; yet their data could not deny that such a relationship could exist. They did find, however, that after the age of nine, seeing death as a universal phenomenon was established. None of the age groups (under six years, six to eight years, and over nine years) showed an understanding of death as being irrevocable. Childers and Wimmer concluded that an awareness of death was not independent of age, although the nature of this relationship was in need of additional research.

Although research on children's concepts of aging has been minimal at best, the material that does exist suggests that the child can learn to equate old age with dying and death. Much work is needed, however, in order to gain an understanding of what "being old" means to the child.

In a fascinating series of studies, Rochlin (1967) explored the play activities of children aged three to five years. Using hidden recorders while he played with each child for a number of sessions. Rochlin concluded that his very young friends behaved in ways described and suggested by Nagy (1948) and Anthony (1973); that is, the play of these children revealed their concerns about futurity and death.

When someone known to the child had died, the child became fearful that others he knew would leave him. This increased awareness and apprehension about being separated from others typified the reponses of children of from three to five years old about death, and could be seen further in their questions about where people go and when they would return. Rochlin felt that the play of children served to help them gain some control over a fearful event or phenomenon. Through play, the child can manipulate and try to minimize his fears. In contrast to the prevailing developmental position of his time, Rochlin took the view that the very young child realizes that death is inevitable and builds defensive play strategies to ward off the effects of this knowledge. This is not to say that the child has an adult view of death, but rather, that he does have an understanding of death and organizes his play and other activities to protect himself against the fears associated with such an understanding.

It is the position of this author that both playing and drawing can help the child best to cope with his fears, for how does one fight it out with an abstraction, especially one that isn't well known or defined? It is much easier to oppose death when it is shaped into a known form, such as a personification. Then, even with all the possible combinations of actions and thoughts that death can come up with, it is still in a form the child can understand and, therefore, is easier to deal with than some horrible demon or transparent vapor. Personified, death stands there for the child to see, outlined and restricted within set boundaries. Ambiguities are reduced, even to the extent that so-called monsters can be humanized.

Children's Drawings: An Introduction and Rationale

It has been recognized that the drawings of children show progressive development, starting with making marks on paper, moving onward to scribbling at the ages of 2 to 3, to organizing these marks into patterns in the form of line drawings at about the age of 4 years, to incorporating descriptive forms into the content of their drawings at about 5 years of age. These descriptive forms are refined from about 7 to 9 years of age, while attempts to represent the visual world, including reproducing what others have drawn, appear at 10 or 11 years. The use of aesthetic principles associated with their particular culture increases between about 11 and 14 years of age.

The process of perception is bound to an individual's psychic existence. Lifton's (1973) term "psychic numbing" reflects this idea, in that impairment of perceptual processing disrupts essential mental functioning and the formation and use of symbols. Exploration of symbolic processing of death then can be a gateway for the discovery of psychic hygiene factors that are related to an individual's ability to cope effectively with life crises.

If we can think of an aspect of an individual's personal symbolic imagery as an anticipation of some future interaction with others in other environments, then an understanding of the development of death concepts is most important over the course of that individual's lifespan. Imagery that suggests ways in which we interact with death certainly needs more intense inquiry. Specific to this point is Klein's (1952) report that early imagery can be traced to the infant's fear of annihilation, while the fear of disintegration, stasis, and separation appear to culminate in adolescence and remain throughout the adult and later years.

Imagery, in particular personification, provides the channels through which the influence of cultural imprinting can be felt, and, as noted by Fiefel (1976), may be strong enough to withstand the onslaught of serious illness and sudden religiosity.

> "Is death a personage, don Juan?"
> "What difference does it make?" replies don Juan.
> Casteneda persists in his questionsing.
> "Was your death like a person?"
> "Death is whatever one wishes. . . . I am at ease with people, so death is a person for me. I am also given to mysteries, so death has hollow eyes for me. I can look through them, they are like two windows and yet they move, like eyes move."
>
> Castaneda, 1972, pp. 190–191

Such symbolic systems must be studied using techniques that are psychologically and psychometrically appropriate; this is of utmost concern when eliciting death-related responses. These techniques are usually referred to as projective tests, such as TAT and the Rorschach, which allow the individual to express a range of cognitive-emotional responses. These methods must "recognize that the scope of man's symbolization provides a link between his biology and history, a link essential if either is to be sustained" (Lifton, 1973, p. 33).

Drawings facilitate open discussions with children about their concerns, and ours, about life and death. This is a most important consideration, in that it has been noted that children tend not to inhibit expressions and thoughts about death as adults do, but develop them in fantasy (Freud, 1955; McCully, 1963; Borkeneau, 1955; Vernon and Payne, 1973). The accuracy of children's fantasies is not as important as the fact that they illustrate their concerns about death-related phenomena. To improve our understanding of and ability to deal with these concerns, both in terms of ourselves *and* our children, attention must be given to children's so-called myth conceptions.

The drawings of children can be thought of in terms of representing universal symbolic truths, which arise either out of combinations of unique and culturally unconscious views of the self in the world, or as representations of specific learned cultural symbols. Of interest is that neither assumption has been supported or rejected by empirical studies. This is not surprising, as intrapsychic processes are not easily reached by empiricism. It is apparent, however, that drawing involves the manipulation of symbols and the organization of these symbols into conceptual systems through cognitive processing.

Drawings are a curious and often mysterious mixture of motor and cognitive development. This results in representations of the world that are both personalized and learned, and have a good deal of psychological value and complexity.

For the very young child, the acts of writing and drawing are hardly differentiated; only with development do these actions become more and more separate functions, and it has been thought that self-criticism may appear earlier in drawings than in writing. This sequence also has been studied in relation to motor development, the directionality of the features of objects portrayed in drawings, and their increasing organization, based upon growing and changing concepts. Perhaps, however, the central theme of this developmental pattern lies in the changing cognitive and perceptual features of the child's view of the world.

Very young children appear to gain satisfaction (affective) from expressing themselves in drawing. At about the age of six years, drawing may serve as a second language for expressing concepts and ideas, or as a last effort to retain the ties to the days of pre-socialized language and thoughts. At this stage, drawings begin to take on a great deal of self-criticism, so much so that they may be forsaken as a frame of reference in favor of the verbal form. This is a time of repression. Whether or not it is accurate, this sequencing of behaviors seems to have great value for researchers, whose work has influenced our present thinking about the assessment of children's drawings.

This sequential view of development and growth also is reflected in the feeling that cultural influences have more impact in the latter, rather than earlier, stages of development. These sequences tend to be seen most clearly in the elaboration of specific features of drawings at varying ages.

Cognitive Concerns

Concepts and cognitions are the processes that act as mediators between the perceptions of the child and his drawing behavior, and are indicative of the dynamic exchanges the child has with his environment. These indications have led us to postulate that the successive states of development are related to changes in cognitive processes and processing.

Cognitive models for explaining the drawings of children have also favored the notion that such drawings depend to a large extent upon *concepts* of objects and life forms, rather than immediate visual images. Drawings therefore, have significance for the child because they represent his subjective perceptions of the so-called objective world. Separation, rather differentiation, of images seems to increase as a function of age or maturation. Usually at about the age of five to eight years, object differentiation tends to influence drawings. As the child develops language faculties, the symbolic images of drawings may be given up for the more easily manipulated verbal forms of expression. It is at this time that language makes its negative side known, for it depresses drawing as a mode of expression. Perhaps the child feels this change more than we have realized; perhaps he feels a further splitting of selves, the feeling of alienation not unknown to adults. The child now tries to integrate his experiences of the world through the use of the symbols of language, rather than in the visual symbols of drawing. His projections of the world are now a series of verbal associations that attempt to dominate the child's earlier preference for the use of visual images.

The child may draw what he knows, rather than what he sees. He may not draw all that he knows but may limit his drawings to those symbolic groupings of importance to him at that time. The child's drawings are a type of cognitive mapping of his world, an insight for others to share in.

The cognitive approach to children's drawings has added some fuel to the debates about the relative value of holistic versus reductionistic analytic strategies. Each has raised problems ignored by the other, yet each group also has noted that the drawings of young children show more of their inductive than deductive development. This emphasis is reversed in later childhood and adolescence, a finding that supports the work of Piaget.

Some discussion, if not controversy, has been centered about the relationship between the drawings of children and their personalities. More recent work has suggested that drawings reveal not only temporary feelings and needs but more enduring qualities of the child, such as personality. Drawings may reflect the child's conceptualized self-image, rather than objective consistency and reality; that is, it is the subjective component that is worthy of study, since it is the child's reservoir of projected psychological values about himself and his world. The drawings of children are not accurate reproductions of the objective world; they are filled with selected elements that are chosen for their importance and meaningfulness.

It is the act of drawing that is an important cognitive event. The period of adolescence often is noted for the conflicts engendered by searching for a mode of expression that can adequately tap their identity crises. Can language serve the adolescent better than drawing? This is a question untested by social scientists, although many reports have described the decline of drawing as a mode of expression for the adolescent. These same reports note the importance of drawing for the expression of feelings at an earlier stage of development.

Drawings can be viewed as symbolic, perceptual measures of expected interactions with the world; and as a way of combining, testing, and changing related concepts. As the child experiences growth and as his interactions with different environments become more frequent and complex, his concepts will go beyond earlier categorizations; this can be seen in his drawings and, in a more stylized form, in his later use of verbal expressions. The synthesis achieved by the elements presented in the drawings of children also can act to reinforce, modify, or change existent concepts, as the drawings now can become part of the child's perceptual world. This line of inquiry has led to the use of drawings as projective inlets into intrapsychic processes, especially affectual-oriented ones. This involves a rejection of objectified analysis, which is based upon perceptual consistencies, and an acceptance of the drawing as a reflection of the individual's interpretation of the world within a context of emotional and cultural influences.

Drawings may become more of a complex of cognitive, affective, and aesthetic properties, more of a projection of the adult world; or they can diminish in complexity or actual usage as the child develops verbal skills that can be used to describe abstractions and perceptions that earlier were more readily expressed in drawing. Buhler (1930) has stated this most succinctly by positing that "the development of language first aids drawing and ultimately defeats it as a mode of expression." Buhler goes on to note that by the time a child can draw more than a scribble (three or four years of age), his graphic presentations already are being influenced by conceptualization, memory, and language.

Drawings at this stage are graphic representations of verbal processes. The rather unorganized nature of such early drawings is seen as representing the stage of language development which is as yet culturally unordered. The work of Stotijn-Egge (1952), with Dutch children who were considered to be metally retarded, and of Shirley and Goodenough (1932) has been used to support the notion that the quality of drawing performance is influenced by the ability of the child to use verbally defined symbols. Children with language problems do draw, but studies indicate that their attempts are at the "scribbling" level rather than at the representative level where drawings contain recognizable objects and life forms.

The Projective Use of Children's Drawings

There has been very little argument about the psychological importance of drawings for children, but the exact meaning of drawings for a particular child or group of children has, of course, led to numerous disagreements.

Goodenough (1926) and Alschuler and Hattwick (1947) noted that drawings are influenced by the child's interests and personality; Lowenfeld (1952), Buhler et al. (1952), Harms (1941), Hevner (1935), Lundholm (1921), England (1943), and Scheerer and Lyons (1947), to name a few researchers, have related the drawings of children to motivation, desires, needs, feelings, and emotional states, with varying degrees of success. The common thread running through these works suggests that the drawings of young children represent feelings and not objective accuracy or reality, and that recognizing the concepts found in such drawings is essential to gaining an understanding of the child's view of the world and his problems coping in that world. No systematic theory or evaluation as yet exists, however, to provide a framework for this position.

Therefore, it is not unusual to find that assessments of drawings tend to show reasonable reliability and low validity. In fact, the more rigorously defined and controlled the study, the lower the validity, especially with respect to the development of personality. This effect could have been predicted by Nunally (1967), Chien (1967), and Argyris (1968).

Symbols and Culture

The elements the child chooses to include in his drawings have meaning to him and designate properties of the environment that he may find interesting, pleasurable, fearful, and so forth. The drawings of children, especially those of younger children, are the child's way of communicating qualities of his world view to others, a visual language transcending and embodying cultural forces. These drawings represent a meaningful perspective to the child that is, in part, determined by cognitive development. The drawings of young children are seen to be simplistic and relatively culture-free, while the drawings of older children show increasing differentiation, complexity, and visual accuracy with respect to adult norms.

Seeman (1934) and Read (1945) have noted that the "whorl," a universal characteristic of the drawings of very young children, seems to evolve into the "stick man," a figure to which various appendages are added. In this way, the circulatory nature of these early images has suggested a Jungian analysis based upon the "mandala." It is an imagery system that recedes with further cognitive growth that stresses linearity, not circularity.

Katzaroff (1910) found that Swiss children favored drawing "miscellaneous objects," houses, and the human figure, in that order. For children up to ten years of age in North America, Maitland (1895) found that the human figure was most frequently drawn. Later studies have confirmed children's preference for featuring the human figure in their drawings, as well as houses, trees, furniture, boats, vehicles, parts of houses, and animals. These studies also have noted that, as children age, their drawings become more refined and detailed. Preferred features of their drawings are more than mere representations; they are meaningful verbal symbols to the child and not reproductions. The drawings of young children may show inconsistencies in terms of proportionality, dimensionality, and spaciality; that is, inconsistencies from an adult point of view. For the child, these so-called inconsistencies may be quite logical. They are also universal, because the very young child is still relatively free of cultural influences.

There have been attempts at comparing the drawings of male and female children with respect to their use of symbols, such as representations of masculinity and femininity (Mott, 1954), or preference for the sex typing of characters (Weider and Noller, 1953; Swensen and Newton, 1955; Sherman, 1958). Some stated that boys drew boys 70% of the time and girls drew girls 90% of the time, and some have examined the complexity of contents and images (French, 1952). Nonetheless, there has been very little in the way of attempts to interpret differences related to the sex of the child (Brown and Tolor, 1957; Berman and Laffal, 1953).

Analysis of Drawings

Analyses of children's drawings have ranged from rather broad classifications of thousands of drawings of a variety of types by boys and girls, both normal and abnormal (Kerschensteiner, 1905), to the narrower classification of the developmental sequence of drawings of the human figure (Rouma, 1913; Marino, 1956), to general classification of the development of the essential features of drawings.

Additional attempts have related the elements of drawing to personal adjustment (the H-T-P test, Buck, 1948), to personality (Wolff, 1946; Wachner, 1946; Brown and Goitein, 1943), to psychoanalytic constructs (Schilder and Levine, 1942), and to emotionality (Reichenberg-Hackett, 1953; Shapiro, 1957), and have been concerned with the reliability of analysis of drawings over time (Gasgrek, 1951).

There have been few factor-analytic approaches to the study of drawings. Those that have been attempted have tended to deal with rating the formal qualities of the drawings (Martin and Damrin, 1951; Lark-Horowitz and Norton, 1960; Stewart, 1955). The factors delineated by these forms of analysis are: age or maturity, balance, quality of line or stroke, style or aesthetic quality, and movement. These factors are further grouped into four major functions: 1) realistic or naturalistic, 2) expressive, 3) skilled or aesthetic, and 4) primitive.

Controversy has surrounded and still follows the issues of whether the child draws all he sees, or all that he knows, or some combination. McFee (1961) has stressed the interactionalist perspective, which tries to account for the contents of children's drawings in terms of their development, environment, perceptions, and intrapsychic factors. This approach contends that drawing, just as much as play, can help the child to deal with concepts about life. It is this viewpoint that has influenced the inclusion of drawings in this book.

Children's Drawings of Death: Ages Three through Five

This section will include:

1. A summary of the response types shown in the drawings of 21 boys and 14 girls
2. Representative answers given by these children to the question, "What happens to people when they die?"
3. Response frequencies to three questions about death
   a. Do you ever think about death?
   b. Does everyone die?
   c. Will you die some day?

4. A conversation with five-year-old Jennifer about death and aging.[1] Figures 2–1 through 2–10 are children's drawings that illustrate the first two items in this list. Figures 2–11 through 2–16 illustrate the conversation with Jennifer.

A Summary of the Response Types Shown in Children's Drawings

The colors most preferred by boys for depicting death were black and red, while girls preferred red and purple. These children used only one color in the majority of their drawings; boys used black and girls used red. All the children were provided with a complete box of Crayola crayons for their drawings.

The physical features recorded by children showed the relative importance of eyes, the mouth, the body, and appendages. The coding system for these features was based upon the work of Goodenough (1926) and Harris (1963) and modified for present purposes. The eyes shown in the drawings were wide open and similar to those of "Little Orphan Annie," and were unbounded by eyebrows. Mouths were set in smiles, not in frowns or anger; bodies were generally ameboid in appearance with stick-like appendages. Nonetheless, these frail limbs provided mobility and hence the character of life. To further add to the humanizing

(Text continues on p. 61.)

[1]The full sample of children (n = 201) ranged in age from 3 years 5 months to 13 years, and resided in the southwestern and central areas of the province of Ontario, and in and around Vancouver, British Columbia. They were asked 1) to draw death (efforts were made to insure that the children drew their pictures independently to avoid the problems of copying of other chidlren's drawings) and 2) to discuss their drawings and feelings about death. The testing sessions were carried out in school settings and in rooms set aside for such testing at nearby universities. Parents were asked to attend these sessions and, in most cases, at least one parent was present, usually the mother. They observed the sessions and did not have discussions with their children until the testing was completed. These sessions lasted approximately 1 to $1\frac{1}{4}$ hours.

Figure 2–1. Freddie (4 years, 2 months): "A horse with a dead man riding on him."

Figure 2–2. Harold (5 years): "A parachute. Someone shot the man. After he died, he fell out of the parachute. Then he went away to the mountain to hide from the bomb."

Figure 2–3. Michele (5 years, 1 month): "A person who is dead."

Figure 2–4. Kelly (5 years, 1 month): "A dead person with sand and dirt because they have to bury them."

Figure 2–5. Peter (5 years, 4 months): "A dead person."

Figure 2–6. Tammy (5 years, 1 month): "A man who is dead."

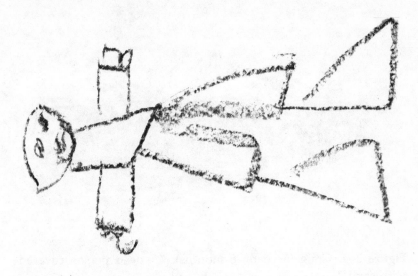

Figure 2–7. Kim (5 years, 4 months): "A person that is laying on the ground dead."

Figure 2–8. Bobby (5 years, 7 months): "A dead person."

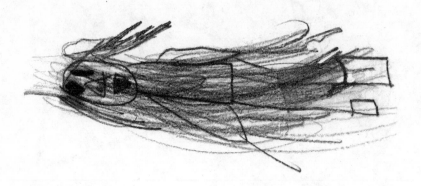

Figure 2–9. Craig (5 years, 6 months): "A dead person covered with sand."

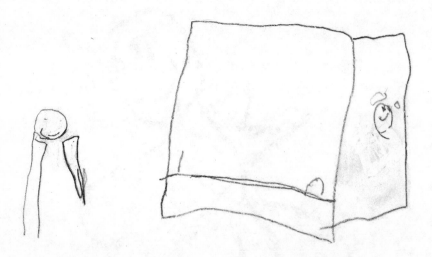

Figure 2–10. Jeff (5 years, 9 months): "A dead person."

elements in the drawings, children gave their life forms hair and even fingers in some cases. Girls illustrated the nose more so than did boys.

Children perceived aspects of death in human and nonhuman forms. Human forms were rather undefined with respect to sex and age. When sexual characteristics made their appearance, masculine traits dominated; in fact, only one child, a female, saw death as a female figure. This finding is supported by the work of Kastenbaum and Aisenberg (1972) and Lonetto et al. (1976) on the perceived sex of death, which reported the overwhelming preference to see death as a male figure.

Although specific activities[2] in these drawings were seldom noted, those that were in evidence showed the dead to be either "standing up" or "lying down." This outcome is, again, in line with previous studies that reported on young children's concerns about sleep versus death, and death as life under changed circumstances. That is, to be dead is to be living, to be standing up, perhaps somewhere else than one's own immediate home environment. One young child handles this "standing up versus lying down" problem by stating that all one has to do is to turn her drawings 90° to give life to the horizontal sleeper or dead person.

Separation themes appeared in the form of being kidnapped, buried, separated from the mother, or in hiding. Killing themes were less frequent, but were in the form of being shot, stabbed, hit by a car, or killed in some undefined way.

The activities recorded by these children suggest that more of their concerns were about the condition of being dead, about whether one is upright or prone, and about separation and abandonment; fewer were about the methods of achieving the status of the dead.

[2]These activity categories were derived from the reports of previous investigators and were used to assess the drawings of children up to 12 years of age. The reader should bear in mind, therefore, the comparisons to be made using these categories. Inter-rater reliabilities for these categories averaged .839.

The specific contents shown in all the drawings collected extend over an imaginative range including parachutes, monsters, cars, and an orange sucker. Some life and death symbols, such as water, flowers, and trees were lacking; yet other such symbols were present, such as rain, thunder, snow, a dog, a horse, and bees (which may have replaced ants as providng the first experience children have with death, as noted by Kavanaugh). Dead persons and animals were found in 60% of the drawings, indicating how these children replace death with the dead. These responses are both suggestive and interesting at this stage of discussion; however, in later chapters these contents will be contrasted with those of older children, in order to form a more integrated view of the symbolic usage and changes in children's drawings. (For a complete summary of the contents of the drawings of these three-to-five year olds, see the appendix of this chapter.)

At this point, the symbols used by three-to-five year olds do not easily lead one to find strong symbolic similarities in their drawings. It may well be that there is no reasonable adult equivalent for understanding this linkage. The child's symbols can be seen as a confusion containing a flux of meanings bonded by temporal, situational or individual forces at times, at other times bonded only by their own dynamics, unrestrained; for children can experience the universe as an inseparable whole including the child himself as an essential feature.

Some Representative Comments Given by Children to the Question: "What Happens to People when They Die?"

Robert, aged 4½: "They have to get buried in the grass. . . . Dead people can't do things because they're dead . . . the body goes away when people die, it breaks apart and goes to heaven."

Elinore, aged 4: "Somebody comes and puts dirt over top and pats it down and puts flowers on it . . . so they can tell somebody is under the ground . . . . Young people don't die . . . maybe when I'm older like grandma."

Michelle, aged 4: "Dead people can't hear or yell or walk. Dead people have their arms and legs out, they can't move . . . must go to hospital and get better."

Jody, aged 4: " . . . can get dead from black monsters . . . they hurt people. . . . People go to doctors when they die. He gives them a needle because they're dead . . . then they have supper . . . you use your car to get home from the doctor's. . . . Oh yeah, bad guys shoot people."

Billy, aged 4: "Death man is old and scary . . . . Ambulance takes dead people to the doctor's and he fixes them up better. . . . dead people can feel."

Kim, aged 4: "She [death] kills people and gets a baby . . . they're killed because they steal money. . . . Go to doctor's when you die [saw it on TV]. . . . You close your eyes when you die . . . you can hear . . . . Police put dead people in jail because they steal money."

The comments made by children about death during their conversations with the authors and members of the study team[3] illustrate that their concerns cover such areas as burial, mobility, aging and death, sensing the world after death, coping with monsters, the consequences of illegal activities, the influence of television, and seeing the hospital and physician as capable of giving life to the dead.

In general terms, these comments are suggestive of beliefs in the cyclical nature of life and death, whether aided by medical intervention or through the birth of babies after death, even the babies of monsters. The comments follow somewhat the animistic notions associated with the cognitions of young children, in that

---

[3]Some comments appear in the previous quotes, while others accompany the drawings of the children.

not being alive can mean immobility with or without functioning sensory apparatus. Thus, the dead for some children cannot hear, while for others they can.

Frequency of Responses Given by Children Aged Three through Five to Questions about Death

	Yes		No	
	Male	*Female*	*Male*	*Female*
a. Do you ever think about death?	3	3	4	1
b. Does everyone die?	2	3	5	3
c. Will you die some day?	2	3	5	1
	7	9	14	5

The responses given by the children to the questions described in the table are similar to those reported by Anthony (1973), Nagy (1948), and Childers and Wimmer (1971), and indicate that

1. There is some confusion about the universality of death.
2. Those children who thought about death only did so at night.
3. Those children who felt that they would die someday stated that death would come only when they were very old, as old as their grandparents.

Death does not come to the young, but to the old.

A Conversation with Five-Year-Old Jennifer

This conversation took place after Jennifer had completed her series of ten drawings (see Figures 2–11 through 2–16). Jennifer then used her drawings to show us what she thought about aging and death. This material is presented as an example of how parents and educators can use the drawings of children as a way of mapping their cognitive concerns. It is by no means to be interpreted as a clinical inquiry. It is a lesson period in which the adult assumes the role of listener and student.

I: What happens when people die?

J: They go with God to heaven and get a new body.

I: How does your body change?

J: I don't know.

I: You said something about castles?

J: Yeah.

I: Where are these castles?

J: In heaven. There's nice castles in heaven and they're all different colors. All of the castles that are in heaven are different colors. [See Figure 2–11.]

I: And you go there after you die and you get a new body?

J: Yeah.

I: You'd like to die in your sleep?

J: That's what I was thinking, only in some of my dreams.

I: What happens in your dreams?

J: You know, I pretend I have a real gun, but it's only a toy gun.

I: And what do you do with this toy gun?

J: Pretend it's a real gun and pretend we're killing people.

I: And what happens to you? Do you get shot from this toy gun?

J: Yeah, but I know I'm not dead.

I: You know it's a dream?

J: Yeah, you know, dreams come from dream boxes.

I: Where are these dream boxes?

J: Under my bed, sort of thing, and there's holes where things, where the dream boxes are that we turn on, and there's tapes in the dream boxes.

I: So you think death might be a he or a she?

J: Yeah.

I: And what does the he or the she look like?

J: Well, like a dumbo to me. [See Figure 2–12.]

I: What's a dumbo? What does a dumbo look like?

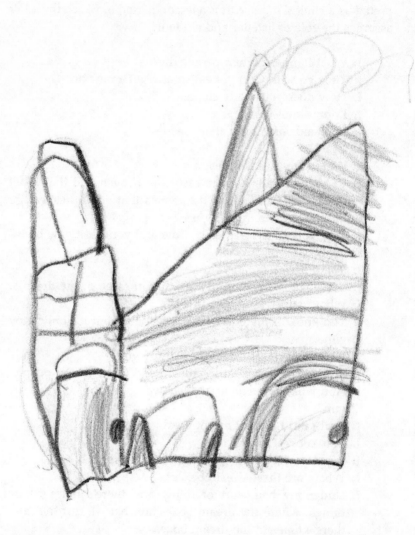

Figure 2–11. Five-year-old Jennifer's drawing of the castles in heaven.

Figure 2–12. Jennifer (5 years): "Death looks like a dumbo . . . a funny clown."

J: It looks like a *funny clown* in my dreams.

I: Do you dream about a dumbo?

J: Yeah and that's what this looks like to me.

I: He looks like a clown?

J: Yeah, he looks like a dumbo.

I: Why do you think people get old?

J: When they grow up they get to be older I think, that's what I think sometimes in my dreams, sometimes in all of my dreams.

I: And what happens to these people as they're growing old?

J: Well, I think in my dreams, things happen to them and they get old.

I: And then what happens?

J: They turn into a cat and chase dumbos away.

I: If you met death, what would you do?

J: Jump on death.

I: And then what?

J: I would tiptoe all over his back.

I: Why?

J: Just to make him ticklish.

I: Do you think death is ticklish?

J: Well, just to make him ticklish, so I could tickle him because I want to.

I: Okay, before we were talking about where you were before you were here.

J: In heaven, in a castle and I had a new body.

I: Then you came here?

J: I was a baby then, and I was about that big when I was a little girl, like mother said that I was about that big and Mildred was about that big, and I was about that big.

I: And you were in heaven before you came here?

J: Yeah, and then I got a new body when I came out of the castle, my other body when I was in the castle was getting pretty old and dirty and so I got a new body.

I: What else happened to your old body besides getting dirty?

J: Oh, you know like some people kept throwing mud on it and throwing hot dogs on it because they wanted to get me all dirty so I would look funny, but I said "Pooey, get all that stuff off me," because I shouted out to everybody who did that and everybody said, "Oh no, I won't."

I: And you say that you had an old body up in the castle?

J: Yeah.

I: And then you got a new body when you came here?

J: Yeah, and then I put a different body on, a baby body on, and I crawled all the way here because babies crawl.

I: Before you said that death was a funny guy too. Isn't that what you said before?

J: Yeah, I think death is a funny guy too. . . . Once upon a time there was a lot of people in a very large family and they all decided to go out but one, and they always used to walk and walk and then they always saw a gun; and then they always ran but they didn't run too fast and the man who was shooting saw them and went "Bang" and then the little girl died from the gun. [See Figure 2–13.]

I: You don't think you always die from a gun, do you?

J: No I don't. If you get very sick, you can die.

I: What else?

J: I don't know.

I: Where do you think you got your idea about people dying by guns?

J: Oh, because I see guns on TV and people shooting guns at people on TV with guns . . . last year, and Mr. Dress-Up is my favorite show.

I: Where else could you go besides heaven when you die?

J: Any place you want to go, by just sliding and jumping up and down and saying, "No, I'm not dead."

I: Can you come back then?

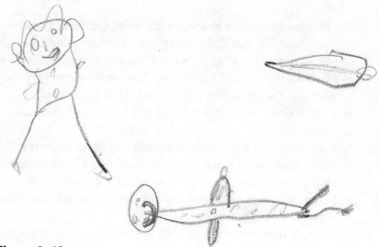

Figure 2–13.

J: As long as you get a new body, as long as you get a baby body and when you're done in heaven.

I: Can you come back as something different than in a baby's body?

J: Yeah.

I: What else can you come back as?

J: You can come back with everything you need to be a baby because you are going to be a baby.

I: Can you be something else besides a baby though?

J: Well, you can be a cat and go "meow, meow, meow."

I: What else can you be in heaven?

J: A dog and go "whoof, whoof, whoof."

I: Can you come back as a cat or a dog?

J: You can come back as anything you want to be.

I: Do you make that choice?

J: Yeah.

I: So you can come back as a cat or a dog or anything that you like?

J: Yes.
I: But you choose to come back as a baby girl?
J: Yeah, as a baby girl . . .
I: Do you think animals die of guns too?
J: I think some do, only if they're supposed to get killed by guns.
I: Are some animals supposed to get killed by guns?
J: I think so.
I: What else do animals die of?
J: Maybe of flu and maybe of poison.
I: And where do animals go, do they go to a heaven like people?
J: Oh, no, they will go to animal heaven. Animal heavens are a lucky place, that's animal heaven.
I: Do bad animals and bad humans go to a different place besides heaven?
J: Bad animals and bad people go to the lucky heaven, it's called the lucky place. It's a heaven too, but I really like the beautiful heaven, because it's called world heaven.
I: What happens to the bad people?
J: They get shot in heaven from guns.
I: Bad people go to heaven too?
J: Yeah, only bad people can only go to heaven to get shot from guns.
I: Why do you talk about guns so much, do you think, because you see so much of it?
J: Of guns?
I: Yes, you talk about guns a lot, don't you?
J: No, only if I want to talk about guns.
I: But everytime I ask you about death, you talk about guns; is that because you see so many guns?
J: Oh no, only in my dreams I see so many guns, only in my bad dreams.
I: You were talking about dream boxes, remember you were talking about dream boxes? Can you dream about death if you pick the right tape to put in your dream box?

J: Only if you have the right money to pay for the tape for death.

I: So you have to pay for your tapes in your dream box?

J: Yeah, in the dream box.

I: And do dreams about death cost more?

J: Oh no, they only cost about one cent.

I: When do you think you're going to die?

J: Oh, I think when I'm done living.

I: And when do you think that will be?

J: Oh, a long time before I want to come back here.

I: Are you going to be old when you die?

J: Oh, I think maybe about fourteen or fifteen, or twenty.

I: Where do you think you will be buried?

J: Under sand, under a lot of sand.

I: In a special place?

J: Yeah.

I: Where?

J: That's where I think I will be buried.

I: Where? Where's the special place?

J: At a place at where you get died from bury people and get died, where people bury other people that get died, are dead.

I: Do you think people will remember you after you die?

J: No, oh I think people will say, "Oh, where's my darling little girl?"

I: So people will miss you?

J: Yeah, I think they will and I never want to die.

I: You don't want to die now?

J: No.

I: I thought you said that you were going to die when you were fourteen or fifteen.

J: Only when I want to die, only when Mommy's going to die.

I: You're going to die when you want to die?

J: Only when my mommy's going to die.

I: Why?

J: Maybe I'll be bigger by then, maybe I'll be as big as my mommy then.

I: What do you think is going to happen to your mommy when she dies?

J: My mommy will get buried.

I: Will she go to heaven?

J: I think so.

I: Have you ever seen death?

J: Only in my dreams.

I: Besides in your dreams?

J: Just only in one dream last year and he was about that big.

I: Did death say anything to you?

J: Oh, he said, "What are a knome and a bome?" and I said, "Knomes and bomes, oh I don't understand," is what I said and then he said, "What are mean old mesknomes . . . ?"

I: Death wanted to know from you what mesknomes were?

J: Yeah and I said, "Don't talk to me and say those kinds of things, say things that I can understand," that I said to death and death said, "Don't back talk." It's not fair to me, death, can't speak what we want death to speak, like only lady deaths can speak what we want death to speak.

I: Only lady deaths?

J: Yeah.

I: Are there lady deaths and men deaths?

J: Yeah, only lady deaths and men deaths and *no boy deaths.*

I: Does death wear a mask?

J: Yeah, masks like this. [See Figure 2–14.]

I: What do they look like?

J: That angry mask. Because death is angry sometimes from people wearing death's masks, that's why death is angry and he's green when he's angry.

I: What else does death wear? [See Figures 2–15 and 2–16.]

J: He wears boots and vamps.

I: What are vamps?

Figure 2–14.

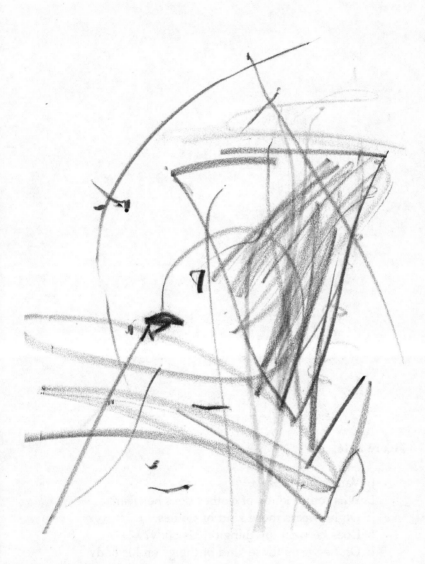

Figure 2–15.

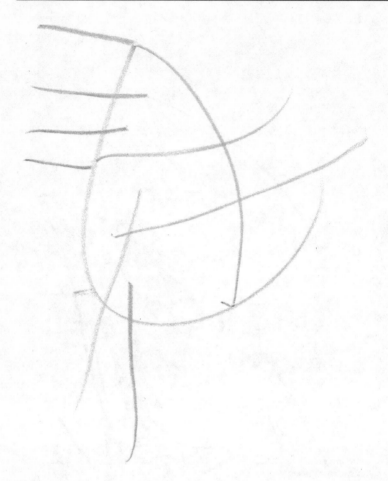

Figure 2–16.

> J: Vamps are those.
> I: What other kinds of clothes does he wear?
> J: Oh he wears those kind of clothes.
> I: Does he wear anything on his body?
> J: Oh he wears those kind of things on his body.
> I: What kinds of things, like what you've got on?
> J: No, those kind of things.
> I: How would you describe those kind of things?

J: Oh just by drawing them and saying them.

I: But if you said to somebody else that you saw death and they said, "What was he wearing?" how would you describe it, besides drawing it?

J: I'd get the picture, and run out if they're still there, and show it to them.

I: Does he wear what everybody else wears or does he wear a gown?

J: No, he just wears what he's supposed to wear.

I: What does he wear everyday?

J: All those things that I drew.

I: Yeah, but what are they made out of?

J: Oh, they're made out of plastic and paper and cloth that's what, the clothes that death wears, what the clothes are made out of . . . and death is *made out of copper.*

I: Does he have skin like you?

J: No, he has copper skin, a whole bunch of copper skin. I'll draw a whole bunch of copper skin.

I: Does he just have skin like yours except darker, or is he metal?

J: No, he's just copper.

I: He's all copper?

J: Yeah, a whole bunch of copper.

I: Can you describe his face to me?

J: Oh, his face is metal.

I: Copper too?

J: No, just metal.

I: What kinds of things does he have on his face? Does he have eyes and a nose?

J: No, he doesn't.

I: What does death eat?

J: He eats doughnuts and meat and he eats hamburgers.

I: Does he have to eat?

J: Yeah and he has to drink too.

Jennifer has made a place after death for both people and animals. She plays with death, personifies death, and holds a discussion with death that displeases her because death has presented her with a riddle to solve which she does not understand. Death is seen as being male at times, female at others, but never as a child. Kastenbaum and Aisenberg (1972) and Lonetto et al.(1976) report similar perceptions, along with death not seen as being fat.

Death for Jennifer can occur only after "Mommy" has aged sufficiently, perhaps when Jennifer has reached the age of 14 or 15 years. This age may mean being old to her, and an age at which separation from mother seems to be more acceptable. She is willing to exchange her "dirty" body for a new one, that of a baby or of some other life form, a viewpoint not unlike the transformation noted in *The Tibetan Book of the Dead*.

Her drawings and conversation demonstrate the strategies she is developing for coping with aging and death. It is in her games with death that we can see the viewpoints expressed by Rochlin (1967) and Maurer (1966): the play of children is their way of coping with their fears. Jennifer is playing a game with the taboo figure of our time, a game that may help her to cope with her anxieties as she grows older.

Conclusions

The drawings of these three-to-five year olds show their concerns about the physical features of death and the dead, the condition of the dead, and separation and abandonment. They are generally supportive of earlier research findings. The drawings seem to suggest ways of dealing with aging and death, and show a tendency toward humanizing the unknown, especially if the unknown takes the form of a monster. Also recorded in their drawings is a good deal of confusion of "the dead" with "death." The drawings of children between the ages of three and five indicate that the methods of dying (by shooting or stabbing) are not as frequently perceived as are the methods of separation (kidnapping, hiding, and so forth) or the condition of the dead (standing or lying down).

The specific contents of these drawings and their themes will be compared later in this book with the drawings of older children, as a way of examining some of the dynamics of expressing concerns about aging and death. The reader is cautioned that, unfortunately, we are not studying the same children as they grow older.

Appendix to Chapter 2

Summary of the Contents of the Drawings of Children Aged Three through Five: Frequency of Responses

Response Type	Males (n = 21)	Females (n = 14)
Colors used		
Black	10	4
Red	6	7
Yellow	2	3
Brown	4	5
Purple	4	7
Orange	3	5
Blue	5	3
Green	2	3
Number of colors used		
1	11	8
2	5	3
3	1	2
4	4	0

Response Type	Males (n = 21)	Females (n = 14)
5	0	1
6	0	2
Physical features		
None	0	0
Hair	7	5
Ears	2	4
Eyebrows	0	1
Eyes: two	11	11
more than two	1	1
Eyelashes	0	1
Nose	4	10
Mouth: smiling	10	11
frowning/in pain	1	1
open	0	0
Neck	3	1
Body: yes	12	8
no	3	3
Navel	1	1
Arms: two	5	8
more than two	0	0
Hands: with fingers	1	4
without fingers	1	3
Legs: two	10	9
more than two	1	2
Feet: two	2	4
more than two	0	0
Gender		
Male	6	3
Female	0	1
Unspecified	10	7
Nonhuman form	7	3
Age		
Infant	0	0
Child	0	0
Adult	3	1
Aged (e.g., grandparent)	0	0
Undetermined	13	5
Actions		
None	0	0
Walking	2	1
Talking	1	1
Watching	0	1
Eyes closed	0	1

Response Type	Males (n = 21)	Females (n = 14)
Smelling	0	0
Sneezing	0	1
Touching	0	0
Standing	7	5
Lying down: in bed	5	2
because of fatigue	1	0
Running	1	0
Hiding	1	0
Digging in the ground	0	0
Funeral services	0	0
Calling for help	0	0
Specific contents		
A blob	3	1
Articles in house	0	0
Bed	0	0
Birds	0	0
Blood	1	0
Bomb	1	0
Buildings (nonspecific)	0	0
Candles	0	0
Casket	0	0
Clouds	0	1
Cross	0	0
Dirt	1	1
Dog	1	0
Electric outlet	0	0
Flowers	0	0
Fork	1	0
Glasses	0	0
Grass	0	0
Gun	0	0
Hats	0	0
Hearse	0	0
Hearts and tears	0	0
Horse	1	0
House	0	1
Hospital	0	0
Insect (e.g., bee)	1	2
Knife	1	0
Mask	0	0
Monster	2	1
Mountain	1	0
Orange sucker	1	0
Parachute	1	0

Response Type	Males (n = 21)	Females (n = 14)
Plane	1	0
Policeman	0	0
Rain	1	1
Shovel	0	0
Sky	0	0
Snake	0	0
Snow	0	1
Squirrel	1	0
Stars	0	0
Sun	0	0
TV	1	0
Tank	0	0
Thunder	1	0
Tombstone	0	0
Trees	0	0
Vehicle (car, ambulance)	2	0
Water	0	0
Windows/doors	0	2
Actions associated with death		
Attacked by a monster	0	0
Attacked by snakes	0	0
Being buried: in the ground	0	2
in a box	1	1
Being scared	0	0
Being separated	0	1
Being sick (e.g., heart attack)	0	0
Bleeding	0	0
Blood sucking (e.g., by a vampire)	0	0
Bombing/war	0	0
Car accident	1	0
Crucifixion	0	0
Electrocution	0	0
Fire	0	0
Hitting	0	0
Hurting	0	0
Kidnapping	0	1
Shooting	2	0
Smoking	0	0
Stabbing	0	0
Not described	17	9

The reader should note that more than one method associated with the death of figure(s) in the children's drawings may be found in each drawing.

3

The Child from Six through Eight Years

Developmental Concerns

The years from six to eight have been termed the "middle years" of the developing child. As has been the case for the middle-aged adult, this age range for children has tended to be thought of as a time for settling and fitting in, especially in relation to physical development. These years signal the onset of the social rehabilitation of the child, which has as its primary objective the building of the superstructures of the adult of the future. It is a process that attempts to take a small being of about 46" in height, weighing approximately 48 pounds, with at least a few missing teeth, and who is busy refining muscular movements, and transform him into an acceptable member of society.

The child still plays and, through play, experiments with the world. This is a point at which the comparison between middle-aged adults and children breaks apart. The middle-aged period of adulthood has been equated culturally with negative emotional, physical, and spiritual states, and with a general lack of activity. The middle years for the child are marked by transitions from home to school, and from family to peers.

Going to School

A great presence begins to exert its influence with increasing force upon the six-to-eight year old. Adults call this presence "the culture"; it can be identified by its specific systems of weights and measures for judging behaviors and thoughts. Perhaps one of its most easily recognized systems is that of formalized education. The education system is one of the most powerful allies of enculturation, for this system houses the sacred and mysterious places for learning the symbols of communication that connect the child to other life forms in the world.

The guiding values and beliefs of formalized learning bring with them feelings of triumph, failure, and change. One might be tempted to introduce school to the child in much the same way as sports are introduced on television. School can be an arena in which the participant can taste "the thrill of victory and the agony of defeat!"

A popular mythology has suggested that school is a training ground for life. There is relatively little supportive evidence for this belief; however, the *social development* of the child is influenced by encounters with classmates and having to deal with the pressures of his peer group. Ideas about the self and of events in the world are expressed, exchanged, and assessed. Through these processes, the child may be confronted with views that are different from those he holds and those reinforced at home. Such communicative experiences can be very confusing, exciting, and often challenging. The child's social environment changes as a result of his contacts with different values and beliefs. It also changes as he moves the center of his activities out of the home and into the school and streets, becoming closer to his peers.

Language is felt to help the child overcome the anxieties of being away from home (Anthony, 1973). The utilization and learning of communicative skills, then, can be a valuable clue to the development of anxieties in the child in the middle years. Let us suggest that the fear of separation is one of the major imbalances of human existence that can be compensated for, and can be reduced to a more comfortable experience through the effective acquisition and use of social language. Social language is used to communicate with others, as opposed to inner language, which is used to communicate with oneself (Vygotsky, 1962). The acquisition and use of this sort of language can be more important for the child who has strong fears about being separated from others than for the child whose fears are not so dominant. These more fearful children could well turn out to be the better learners, as seen by their parents and teachers. These children also could find great rewards in adopting the adult or peer role models associated with the reduction of separation fears, greater rewards than children who deal with separation without such high levels of fear.

Going to school may be looked upon as a primary testing ground where the child can seek out the dimensionality of his feelings about himself, including his feeling for autonomy. There is somewhat of a paradox here, in that, while the child gradually is learning to deal with the demands for conformity placed upon him by significant others in his social environment, he also is trying to find "himself."

The forces acting on the six-to-eight year old can further be found in the way they criticize their own performance of socially approved tasks. Children adopt self-criticism along with behavior directed toward autonomy and responsibility. Our view of this development is that without self-criticism the chances of completing the jigsaw puzzle of the self are not very good, yet little mention is made of the role played by attitudes of self-acceptance. Cannot self-criticism, without benefit of acceptance and integration, be destructive to the growth of the self? We seem to have neglected the influence of self-acceptance and its relationship to criticism of the self.

The development of concepts about the self also requires that appropriate male and female identities will be selected and internalized by boys and girls. Early school experiences serve as strong reminders of socially appropriate sexual behaviors (Minuchin, 1965; Rains and Morris, 1969). Going to, and being in, school tends to subdue the range of emotional expressiveness displayed by children when they are younger. School presents adult mores to the child, with their reward and punishment contingencies. This is indeed interesting, as some descriptions of six year olds given by psychologists and sociologists show the child to be faced with many socially oriented stresses (separation, peer pressures, success and failure) that turn his life into cycles of turmoil and contentment as he tries to fit into the expanding world. There are, of course, other descriptions that focus more on the comforting aspects of fitting in.

The range of the emotional world of the child can be seen in the fears associated with six year olds, which have been reported to include 1) the forces of nature (rain, thunder, lightning, wind), 2) the supernatural (ghosts, witches, monsters, strange shapes), and 3) associated auditory and visual phenomena (loud noises, someone hiding either in a closet or under a bed who is obviously up to no good). Seven and eight year olds may show fears of events related to the self. This does make sense, as these older children are becoming increasingly aware of the social image they project. Their fears about the self reflect some of the traumas of the social environment, such as failing at school, losing the approval of peers, appearing too successful in relation to peers, being criticized by others, and feeling different from peers.

These children are showing concern about deviations from learned social norms and are beginning to realize the impact of the sanctions connected with behavioral or cognitive deviations. The knowledge of self acquired by the child as he passes through the educational system should lead him to choose an acceptable role, rather than an antisocial one. It is taken for granted that no child gets through the system without being transformed in some way.

I found that they [my schoolmates] alienated me from myself. When I was with them, I became different from the way I was at home . . . . It seemed to me that the change in myself was due to

the influence of my schoolfellows, who somehow misled me or
compelled me to be different from what I thought I was.

Jung, 1977, pp. 34–35

Language and Thought

The most notable cognitive development for the six-to-eight year
old is his introduction to the mysteries and usefulness of the
alphabet. This is the beginning step in the formal learning of
communication symbols and the consequent submerging of personalized (internal) symbolic structures in favor of socialized (external) ones.

The child of four to seven years of age, according to Piaget
(1952a), is in the interactive phase of cognitive growth. This is a
phase characterized by the child's ability to think in terms of
classifications of subjects and perceived relationships between
them. yet children tend to remain aware that they are imposing
an order on the objective world. This phase marks for the six year
old a change to asking "why" rather than "what" questions.

During the years from 7 to 11, the child is able to employ the
rules of logical inquiry (including the notions of reversibility and
sequential classifications) and is said to be in the phase of concrete operations. The child is seen as being capable of solving
manipulative problems, such as can be touched, seen, and re-
ordered. Concrete operational thought appears as the precursor
to the next phase of development in which the child acquires the
ability to deal with problems of a more abstract nature that require some understanding of time and space.

The six year old is said to be at the level of reasoning where he
is unable to make room for cause and effect relationships, but he
can allow the perceived physical properties of objects to affect his
decisions about their similarities or differences. Seven year olds
are reported to be concerned about the principles of conservation,
which stress the constancy of the properties of objects. The eight
year old makes attempts to escape from the concrete into the
abstract while continuing to explore the jungle of causal relationships. The issues and efforts surrounding the turning from the

concrete to the abstract remain, to a large extent, unexamined. Is it that the child simply loses enthusiasm for the obviousness of the empirical inquiries he enjoyed during the concrete phase of development, and begins to look for much more enlightened views?

Play and Morality

Fantasy and physical activities combine in the play of children even as other forces are at work changing the character of play. A major shift in the play of an eight year old from that of a five year old is the separation of the sexes, which signals the growth of concerns about group-oriented games and the types of play that call for companionship and secrecy (as found in the formation of secret clubs). Jung (1977) noted the possession of a secret had a most powerful effect on the development of his character. Secrets were considered, by Jung, to be essential factors in his boyhood.

The younger child's unitary view of the world cracks somewhat or may even shatter with the separation of boys and girls in play activities. This separation can lead to affairs of the heart between boys and girls who are going through this type of change. An unfortunate side effect of segregation by sex in play is that the child may place a good deal of emphasis on the achievement of social acceptability as a method for coping with separateness, and thus come to value certain activities simply because they make different demands on boys and girls. Furthermore, children may even lose interest in certain activities because of their association with a specific sex group and will engage in them only if they are properly rewarded, for instance, if they are paid for the performance of tasks around the house.

Piaget (1960), Maurer (1966), and Rochlin (1967) observed children at play as a way of discovering the child's view of the world. Through play, children learn to cope with their personal devils; the rules of their games yield clues to their views of morality, including the treatment of violators of rules. For the young child, the rules of play are absolute, perfect, and correct. Transgressors are guilty of committing a major offense. With the passage of a few years, offenses are no longer interpreted strictly from a quantitative standpoint, but are open to interpretations with regard to the intentionality of the offensive action. The orginal set of rules are a precise, correct guideline for honest behavior, but as the child matures the rules become capable of misapplication and being in error. What were once simple decisions about deviations from fair play now are influenced by extenuating circumstances. The rules of games undergo a transformation paralleling that of the cognitive growth of the child, moving from a perfectly understood awareness of the unity of the objective and subjective world to a relative and less perfect awareness.

The moral development and dilemmas of children are felt to be an essential aspect of play and are a complex of cognitive, environmental, and unique personal factors, the exact nature of which is not comprehended clearly. Although considerable effort has gone into examinations of these concepts (Gesell and Ilg, 1946; Piaget, 1960; Almy, Chittenden, and Miller, 1966), the same cannot be said about studies of the differences between what constitutes morality for the child and what is acceptable to and for adults; nor of the effects on the development of the child and of society that are created by discrepancies between child and adult views of morality.

The middle years of childhood are believed to encompass the time in which the child begins to become acquainted with God, a powerful, humane, and punishing figure who has even more authority than his parents.

Children's Concepts of Death: Ages Six through Eight

Nagy (1948) reported that children between the ages of five and nine personified death and identified death with the dead, keeping death at a reasonable distance so that they would have time for an escape. These views represent a reshuffling of the cognitions about death held prior to five years of age, which made death a reversible, temporary change, a living on under changed circumstances.

Nagy asked children to respond to the question "what is death?" in composition and/or discussions. In their compositions, approximately 92% of seven and eight year olds (n = 36) either showed death to be a separate being, or merged death with the dead; while no five year old saw death in similar ways. The remaining 8% of the children felt death was a kind of process that obeyed certain defined patterns; this is a perceptual characteristic that has become associated with older children. Somewhat varying results were obtained from discussions about death: 44% of the seven-to-eight year olds were concerned about death as a process.

In Nagy's study, children's personifications of death contained most of the following trait descriptions, either singularly or in combination:

> Death is scary, frightening, disturbing, dangerous, unfeeling, unhearing, and silent. Death takes you away. If you see death coming at you in time, you can escape. Death can be invisible like a ghost or ugly like a monster or it can be a skeleton. Death can be an actual person, or companion of the devil, a giver of illness, or an angel.

These descriptions of death provide examples of how personifications can help children to cope with death. The once-invisible skeleton is rendered visible and the child now can escape from its grasp. Through personifications, children can locate, identify, and, of great importance, elude death.

Nagy found that about one-third of the children's personifications transformed death into "the dead," in much the same way as death appeared in the drawings of three-to-five year olds presented in Chapter 2. Death also was associated with the aged and the sick.

The often-invisible spirit of death seems to have a slight tendency to travel about in the evening. Fifteen percent of the children said that they thought about death in the evening, and that it was usual to die at night.

Personifications not only make death visible but also humanlike in appearance. This visibility can be for just a brief time before death carries a person off. If one acts quickly, this is just enough time to outmaneuver death. Therefore, death can assume a variety of external roles and can occur only when someone is caught by the "death-man." It then makes a good deal of sense, from the viewpoint of the child who personifies death, that the aged and infirmed are hardly in a good position to run away or hide from death, even if they can "see" death. In contrast, the young and the healthy can and do escape from death.

This discussion brings back some memories of the days when we played stickball in the streets of New York City. The playing field was carefully mapped out by sidewalks, fire hydrants, sewer covers, trees, and parked cars. The particular street we played on had an interesting feature that became part of our outfield—a four-way intersection controlled, not by traffic lights, but by stop signs. When a ball was hit to the outfield, the lone outfielder would run to the sewer cover in the middle of the intersection, waving cars away from him. He would stand on that spot and, with a rhythmic display of arm movements known only to street players and the motorists who traveled through and interrupted the game, bring all traffic to a complete halt. Quickly, he would continue on to make a great catch, to a mixture of applause and curses from the drivers in the immediate area. This part of the outfield was called "death alley" and was played by only the youngest and fastest of us.

Safier's (1964) study of 30 boys aged four to ten years gave some support to Nagy's findings, in that it pointed out that six-to-eight year olds saw both life and death as capable of being given and taken away by an external agent. Safier (1964) also noted that the ages of seven to eight for boys were a transitional stage in thinking and asking questions about death, but basic to this stage was the externalization and personification of death. This work represents a way of synthesizing the notions of Piaget and Nagy, as it tends to utilize, in order to adequately describe the child's views of death, stages that seem to be a mixture of cognitive developmental orientations.

For Piaget (1966), the child in the middle years finds death to be a great bewilderment and asks questions about what causes death, for death must have a cause—surely it doesn't just happen by chance! Piaget sought a bond between death-related concepts and the development of the search for causes. This shift toward seeking causal explanations is seen in the child asking "why" rather than "what" questions.

Kane's (1975) research, expanding Piaget's study of children's thinking to include their concepts of death, concluded that by the age of seven years children acquire ideas about death similar to those commonly held by adults. She also noted that by the age of six years the child has added to his death concepts the components of causality, dysfunctionality, universality, and irrevocability. Death for the children in Kane's study was a feature of old age and, therefore, very far away.

Another study that attempted to join Piagetian development with other cognitive maps was that of Klingberg (1957). The writings of Huang and Piaget were used as a background against which an examination was made of how 97 Swedish children aged seven to ten years ascribed life to nonliving forms and how tightly their animistic interpretations were bound to the chain of development described by Piaget. Klingberg concluded that children associate movement with living more than with life, and that Piaget's developmental theory was not quite correct in equating animistic conceptualization with primitive mental functioning. In place of this theory, animistic views could be seen as being influenced by a joint matrix of environmental and educational factors. Perhaps the real importance of this work is not found in the results alone but in its refusal to compress such findings into predetermined cognitive systems.

Koocher (1973), however, did not find that personifications were preferred by children for describing death. It should be noted that Koocher asked children 1) "What makes things die?" 2) "How do you make dead things come back to life?" 3) "When will you die?" and 4) "What will happen then?" Koocher did attempt to show that the child's conception of death is related more to developmental age (mental age assessed via Piagetian methods) than chronological age. As stated in the introduction to this book, the chronological age of children can serve as a guideline for predicting changes in the death concepts of children, since these changes can be seen as products of complicated maturational and sociocultural influences. These may not be that different from the matrix of influences mentioned by Klingberg.

Koocher criticized the work of Nagy and Anthony for their methodological limitations and lack of generalizability but makes no mention at all of similar problems with the work of Piaget. In addition, he laments the lack of good, clear, hard empirical investigations of children's conceptions of death without seeming awareness of the rather severe limitations such methods impose on complex human issues. Perhaps, the question that should be explored first is "empiricism for what?"(Argyris, 1968).

Childers and Wimmer (1971) found that after the age of nine years children understood the universality of death, but as yet had not extended this reasoning to include the idea of the irrevocability of death. Twenty-two percent of the six year olds, 61% of the seven year olds, 75% of the eight year olds, and 100% of the nine year olds gave positive answers to the questions "does everyone die?" and "will everyone die?"

One of the questions asked of children by Koocher (1973) was "when will you die?" In 1934, Schilder and Wechsler formulated the viewpoint that children do not forecast their own death because aging, in particular "being old," has no personal meaning for them. Rather, death is a deprivation, a state related to a punishing agent. Mitchell (1967) reached a similar conclusion when she reported that death was seen as a major deprivation by children. Koocher, however, hypothesized that more realistic estimates of one's future death would appear with increasing levels of cognitive development. Out of the 75 children who were tested, aged 6 to 15 years, 23 six-to-nine year old boys and girls gave responses that fell within the preoperational and concrete operational levels, with only one girl in the 8-to-9 year old range fitting in at the level of formal operations. The mean age of the preoperational group was 7.4 years; it was 10.4 years for the group at the concrete operational level. The age range for children who were classified as being at the level of concrete operations was 6 to 13 years.

All but one child predicted their age of death. Such predictions ranged from 7 years (given by a six year old) to 300 years (given by a nine year old). The 20 children in the preoperational group gave an estimate of 86.6 years (standard deviation = 66.01); the children at the concrete operational level predicted that they would live, on the average, 81.3 years (standard deviation = 12.68). Koocher goes on to say that these results are "a dramatic example of the importance of the reciprocity skills that come with the onset of concrete operations" (p. 74). This may be one of the few times that standard deviations have achieved such recognition, other than in their more usual role of suggesting whether or not samples have been drawn from the same population.

Children believe that children are not supposed to die! Old age is the insidious, death-causing villain, revealed to the child by parents. The death of a parent or grandparent most often is said to be due to age, but what is said to a child when another child has died? Age-related arguments would not be of much use (Schilder and Wechsler, 1934); after all, people don't die until they are at least 100 years old. The world of childhood is eternal in its quality; only with aging can we experience the movement away from this time and, with it, death.

Anthony (1973, p. 155) presents the case of a small girl who wanted to place a large stone on her head so that she could not grow up, become old, and die. If old age *causes* death, as parents have told their children, is it any wonder that we continue to have an adult society that fears aging and cherishes youth? We have created a terribly inhumane story, one that seems improbable to the young child who lacks an adultlike understanding of time. For the child seeking causal explanations of why death occurs, stories linking aging and death can produce a great fear of growing old because aging is seen to be the major cause of death.

Anthony's (1973) work indicated that children eight years of age and younger do not have, by adult standards, logically or biologically correct concepts about death, and that children from seven to eight years old are at a crucial point in their development of death-related concepts. Safier (1964) had similar findings. The children at these ages gave definitions of the word "dead" that gave evidence of comprehending what death means. Of importance here is that the responses of children five years and younger showed no such comprehension; instead, they showed an interest in death along with "limited and erroneous concepts" (Anthony, p. 49).

The older children's responses were descriptive of what Anthony has called the "C-Stage" of development. It is at this stage that children appear to be preoccupied with both personal and culturally sanctioned rituals associated with the dead. The ceremonies of the burial become functions to be imagined, feared, or attended to, whether the dead be human, animal, or insect. For example, Anthony (p. 110) postulated that, until the seventh year, children may enjoy killing small animals and insects (even Jung was fascinated with the slaughtering of a pig); after this age they seem to derive more enjoyment out of playing with and observing animals than by cutting them up or stamping on them. Children who give essentially correct but limited information about death (D-Stage with the lowest mental age of eight years, nine months) can also act out elaborate funeral ceremonies for animals and become increasingly concerned about similar rituals for humans.

We should like to add to this discussion the definitions of the word "dead" given by Catholic school children 7 to 8 years old (n = 62). The predominant response, given by 26 of the children, described death as being the start of a new life in a heaven that is full of love, happiness, and peace. Such responses tend to represent the views expressed by their priests and in their religion classes. Eleven of the children equated death with being killed by an external agent, 6 children associated death with feelings of sadness, and 5 with funeral and burial rites. Only 2 children saw death as being ill, and 1 child felt that death meant "never being ill." Suicidal actions were found in the definitions of death given by 2 children. Table 3–1 presents the frequencies for the full range of definitions given by the children.

These children did not use personifications in defining being dead, but did incorporate their religious training into such responses. From conversations with their teachers, it seems apparent that these children have not been taught about life or death in other than religious terms. Such responses, therefore, are somewhat more reflective of the training received by these chil-

Table 3–1
Frequency of Responses Given by Sixty-two Catholic School
Children, Aged Seven to Eight, When Asked to Provide
Definitions of the Word "Dead"

Response	Frequency
A new life in heaven, one of happiness, love, and peace	26
To be killed by some external agent: hanging, fighting war, and so forth	11
Sadness	6
Funerals, graves, and burial	5
To kill oneself	2
To be sick	2
Never to be sick	1
To be poor	1
To feel hopelessness	1
To hate someone	1
The devil	1
The death of a family member, for example, a grandmother	1
Not to live forever	1
To be real old	1
Something bad	1
Something people don't like	1

dren than of their internalized beliefs about death. In this way, it is of some worth to note that only one child saw death in terms of being old, for it was expected that many more would perceive the union of aging and death.

Borkeneau (1955) found the signs of an emerging cultural interest in death by studying the art and practice of burial rites of the middle paleolithic period. The fact that similar interests are to be associated with the period of middle childhood supports Recapitulation Theory, which compares individual development with cultural development. The strengthening of interest in the ceremonies for the dead also is thought to indicate an increase in awareness of personal mortality. On a historical-cultural level, this argument is presented by Borkeneau; yet we also will see that the awareness of mortality of the self, planted in middle childhood, begins to flourish in the time of later childhood (9 to 12 years of age). At this later time, the orientation of the self in the world stresses that death is a singular event that marks an end to life. The earlier view holds that life and death are cyclical phenomena, with neither capable of being terminated.

Concerns about the rites of burial also can be seen as gauges of the uncertainties felt about the relationship between life and death; thus, the rites are developed and utilized to 1) keep the dead separate and away from the living and 2) to present a sense of life after death which, at one extreme, attempts to insure a static immortality housed in associated monuments and awards. Burial rites have had as their cultural focus a series of prescribed, often elaborate actions aimed at simplifying the nature of a postpartum existence. For example, in the later paleolithic period, burial rituals reflected conceptions about the inevitability of death rather than life after death (Borkeneau, 1955). This conception is shown in striking detail on the black-grey headstones and burial markers, inscribed with skull and crossbones, in the cemeteries of Protestant churches in Scotland. A more dramatic example of the relationship between the living and the dead can be found in the city of Edinburgh, where one of the grandest hotels overlooks a somber cemetery in what is called the "dead center of the city."

The young child, in contrast to accepting and fearing the inevitability of death, is said not to understand death and so denies it. The difficulty here is how one can deny something not conceived of. The denial stage passes with time; as societies and children mature, a viewpoint arises in which death is externalized, defied in some cases, and avoided (running away from the 'death-man'). It then may be suggested that the middle age of a culture, and of childhood, represents levels of development of death concepts that mark a transition from a cyclical view of life and death to one in which death is externalized, recognized, and, it is hoped, eluded.

Summary and Conclusions Regarding Death Concepts

Death for the child from six to eight years old is personified, externalized, and can be avoided if one sees death in time. Death is not yet finalized; rather, it assumes various external forms (skeletons, ghosts, the death-man). The child is expressing a conceptual belief that places emphasis on the separation of internal and external agents. During these years, the child also shows concern about the ceremonial rites associated with the dead. Interest and anxiety appear about funerals and burials.

Nagy's first two developmental stages show movement from a perception of death as a gradual, temporary state of affairs to a concept in which death is personified and externalized. Anthony regards as important the change from having little understanding of the meaning of "being dead" to searching for and employing causal and logical explanations. These shifts have been both supported and reinterpreted by other investigators (Schilder and Wechsler, 1934; Safier, 1964; Koocher, 1973; Childers and Wimmer, 1971; Kane, 1975), but most of the researchers have a common bond, which is a predisposition to see the development of death-related conceptions within a framework stressing linear, rather than nonlinear, stages of development. In general, these stages begin with a refusal to accept the finality of death and move on to death being seen as an external agent. This phasing is completed when death is seen as a termination. It almost seems that the stages have become too important, and certainly more important than their underlying dynamics. Stages, phases, levels, and other categories are becoming our archetypical way of dealing with complex human issues. If the problem can be reduced enough, the illusion is created that it is solved.

It may well be that the lack of systematic relationships found between the child's conception of futurity and death is more a signal of the sophistication of their world view, rather than the immaturity assigned to their views by others who are bound by their notions of the passage of time (see Kavanaugh, 1972). It is only after the child has given up a cyclical concept, in favor of a linear and terminal view, that relationships between concepts of time and death begin to coalesce.

Time is first perceived by children in relation to the ends, not the beginnings, of things. This time perspective will change to incorporate past, present, and future considerations, but basically time will be structured. The internal, nonlinear time of the young child begins its journey to the outside world and yields control of the passage of time to other forces, which can actually cause time to be lost. In the period of internal time, there was control of time through the unity of the child with his world; therefore, there was no death, only changes. With the coming of external time, animals and people age and become disfigured, ill, and even die.

Psychologists, in particular, place a good deal of importance on the perceptions of consistency as clues to cognitive maturity. The feeling seems to be that, when a total lack of variability is perceived, the individual has achieved the highest level of cognitive functioning. Both the modern physicist and Eastern philosopher, however, have joined to tell other scientists that there is no stasis, for the more at rest an object seems, the faster its components are moving. Suzuki (1963) has said that we may *choose to believe* that there is constancy and stillness only, but this does not represent the order of nature.

The assessment of attitudes and conceptions is then a function of the perspective of the observer. One person might see the activity, but others might see nothing at all. Behaviors, or predictions of events, are then to be seen as the probability of an occurrence at a specific location or range of locations. There can never be an absolute certainty in physics or psychology. These probabilities are "maps," not the "territory" of cognitions. We have known all along what being a good observer requires; being in the right place at the right time with the right perspective. Accordingly, the "right perspective" taken by our modern physical scientists is that time and space cannot exist independently; that time is truly a relative term, as demonstrated by the "twin paradox"[1] which attempts to show that time passes in relation to the observer of its passage. The mapping of an event, then, is required only when the observer feels separated from it. Surely this is the case with our studies of the world of the child. We have become strangers in their world and they have not yet learned of ours.

The Fear of Death: An Affective Response

Affective responses to death have been considered keys to the understanding of the child's conception of death and of himself. The literature containing references about these responses is of a varied and confusing mixture at best. There is far less written about the child's views of futurity and death, as tradition has dictated that we should wait for the child to reach early adolescence, when his notion of time is presumed fixed.

The affective response to death that has been subjected to study most often is the fear of death. This fear is thought to be universal (Fiefel, 1959; Hinton, 1967; Swenson, 1961; Zilboorg, 1943), instinctive (De Dellarossa, 1965), a castration anxiety

---

[1]Time intervals have been found to depend on the frame of reference for measurement. This paradox reveals that clocks and even the human heart when in motion, run slower. Time is said to slow down. For example, if one of two twins went on a round trip into space, he would be younger than his twin on earth when he returned, because his heartbeat and his other regulatory systems would have been slowed.

(Chadwick, 1929), fear of pain and the unknown (Kotsovsky, 1939; Von Hug Hellmuth, 1965), terrifying (Chadwick, 1929), a neurotic reaction associated with feelings of helplessness (Freud and Burlingham, 1943; Freud, 1957), a schizophrenic reactive response (Blum and Rosensweig, 1944), related to fears of the dark (Caprio, 1950), fear of suffocation (Harnik, 1930), and is considered to be a rare phenomenon in childhood (Schilder and Wechsler, 1934). It is also thought to represent a separation anxiety for the child under the age of seven years, which can take the form of an aggressive response in the older child (Portz, 1965).

The series of works just mentioned holds valuable information about the child in the middle years. The contributions of Caprio (1950) and Kotsovsky (1939) are particularly noteworthy because they attempt to find links between the fear of death and the emotional influences brought to bear on the child by 1) funeral and burial rites; 2) parental superstitions about the rites; and 3) the guilt and disappointment associated with not fulfilling one's potential, whether self- or other-evaluated. Feelings of guilt and disappointment are also the companions of the child as he enters into and continues through the periods of self analysis and criticism that are felt to be crucial to his pattern of maturation.

It should be mentioned here that Caprio (1950) linked the fear of death to fear of loss of a loved one and to fear of the rituals of the burial. This leads to the suggestion that ghost stories and attendance at funerals produce neurotic fears in adulthood. Children should be told about death only when they are capable of understanding, yet no magic age is presented when this instruction can begin.

The fear of death also has been associated with the fear of loss of the self, the ultimate narcissistic fear (Harnik, 1930; Monsour, 1960); and fear of the threats imposed by other more magical selves, such as by ghosts who represent a living form of a corpse (Becker and Bruner, 1931). For Mitchell (1967), this fear of death was related to and different from the fear of dying. She felt this fear was deeply emotional and was a form of the basic fear of separation, of possibly dying alone. The fear of death has been socialized to some extent by the belief that, in order to achieve positive integration of the self, attitudes toward death must be reviewed and assessed. The fear of dying then becomes associated with the anxieties brought about by knowing that one's work will go unfinished and immortality be denied.

Anthony probably came as close as anyone can to expressing the Westernized view of the fear of death when she remarked that this fear was a disguised version of the fear of the retaliation of others. She presented two distinct streams of this death-related fear: 1) an anxiety which, for the child of five years and younger, centers about feelings of dependency and of aggressive thoughts and actions, and which does not require an adultlike understanding of death, and 2) a critical type of anxiety derived from feelings of being an independent entity but one that is vulnerable and can be ripped from the world by external forces.

With this collage of ideas about affective responses to death, we come to the study done by Alexander and Adlerstein (1958). Their laboratory contained word association tests and instruments to assess GSRs (galvanic skin responses). Their subjects were 108 boys aged 5 to 16 years, 28 of whom were between 6 and 8 years. The children's responses to death-related words, in general, showed an increased latency and a decreased skin resistance. The 5-to-8 and 13-to-16 year olds manifested significant decreases. The 9-to-12 year olds failed to show reliable changes. Alexander and Adlerstein interpreted these results using an ego development model that held that death has greater emotional significance for those with less stable ego structures than for those who have managed to conform their self-concept to socially appropriate structures. In this way, 6-to-8 year olds are in a period of searching for the self, including making adjustments to peer and family demands. This search shifts in its emphasis toward looking for causal-logical explanations for behavioral and emotional phenomena. The 13-to-16 year olds are described as being involved in a redirection of libidinal forces; in contrast, the world of the 9-to-12 year olds is characterized by latency and complacency.

The ages six through eight might be considered a time of initial crisis about the self and might be an early preview to the crises of marriage, middle age, divorce, and retirement that appear in later life. Alexander and Adlerstein (1958) reached a conclusion somewhat along these lines in their statement that, although there is nothing particular to childhood in terms of emotional reactions to death, there are some periods of growth that are characterized by stress and change. The child aged six through eight can be found enclosed by such a period.

Children's Drawings of Death: Ages Six through Eight

Response Types Shown in Children's Drawings

In my work with them, children of both sexes preferred the use of reds, blacks, browns, and, to a lesser extent, purple. These children used multiple color combinations in their drawings of death. This contrasts with the monochromatic drawings of the younger children discussed in Chapter 2.

It is evident from the drawings that the children were concerned with both personifications of death and the ceremonies associated with the dead. Twelve boys and 6 girls personified death, while 8 boys and 13 girls expressed their views on the rites of burial of the dead. There was still some confusion of "death" with the "dead": 4 boys and 8 girls represented death as being a dead person or animal. The children's personifications gave masculine characteristics to death; this tendency does appear at an earlier age. (For a complete summary of the contents of the drawings of these children, see the appendix to this chapter.)

The children showed such features as hair; eyes (only 2 and not more); the nose; the mouth (shown smiling more often than frowning, showing pain, or just being open); two arms (which did not always end in hands with fingers); and two legs (not always completed by feet). Eyebrows, eyelashes, and the neck are not drawn frequently by these older children. Their personifica-

Figure 3–1. Freddie (8 years, 4 months): "Death is a guy who has one eye and one no eye, one arm and a half an arm. His hair is sticking up and he's frightening. He has a cut on his face. One half his body is brown, one half is blue, he stands on little spikes."

Figure 3–2. Joey (8 years): "Death is a man with three heads. He is the person who makes you die. He is frightening and if you see him you get scared."

tions are clothed, thus removing from immediate view the belly button, the direct link with the mother. The characters tend to be of an undetermined age, at least in the judgment of our raters.

No child drew death or the dead as an infant; however, girls and little boys were drawn. As mentioned earlier, Kastenbaum and Aisenberg (1972) and Lonetto et al. (1976) reported that death is not seen as an infant or as being fat by adults. This perspective was found in the drawings of these six-to-eight year olds as well. Although the dead are shown to have smiling rather than pained or tormented expressions, the survivors can be saddened by death.

It should be remembered that when we are examining the nature of children's conceptions of death we need not believe that their expressions on paper are absolute or accurate cognitions of what death is to them; rather, we should look upon these expressions as links to the inner experiences of children.

Historical Perspectives

Personifications of death have historically provided channels for the expression of individual emotional and cognitive orientations toward death, while mirroring specific societal values. One of the oldest, if not the oldest, work on representations of death is Gotthold Ephraim Lessing's essay *Wie Die Alten Den Tod Gebildet* (How the Ancients Represented Death), written in 1769. In the illustrations accompanying the text, death is represented by birds, butterflies, or as a beautiful winged and youthful creature, often human and male. Turning to the contemporary social sciences, Slater (1963) stated that whichever sex seems the more powerful in a particular society will appear most frequently in death personification. In North America, death is more frequently seen as a male figure by children and adults of both sexes (Kastenbaum and Aisenberg, 1972; Lonetto et al., 1976). The sex differences associated with death personifications have included a tendency in adult females to find death somewhat more sexually arousing than males (Osis, 1961; McClelland, 1963; Greenberger, 1965; Paris and Goodstein, 1966). Unfortunately, no clearly defined body of knowledge has appeared in the psychological literature as to the effect on personifications of death made by such factors as age, religion, self-concept, health status, and the like. The studies of adults that do exist have focused on females more so than males, and on the ill more than the healthy (Osis, 1961; Greenberger, 1965).

Who Did What to Whom and How?

In most instances, a man died in the drawing. The children did show that older people died (grandmother, grandfather, great grandmother), but, more important, children of both sexes were shown to be dead. Children of this age may be feeling for the first time the possibility of their own mortality, since their drawings now show that a child, not unlike themselves, can die.

Specific deaths were recorded by the drawings. Examples included the death of a student, of a child's father, and of a friend. Although some of the children discussed the death of a pet as part of their response to "what happens to people when they die?," only one child drew the death of an animal.

The children did not represent frequently the "who" responsible for a death in their drawings. When this "who" was present, it took the form of men killing other men and a girl with the "death-man" killing little boys. A vampire and snakes were additional and externalized agents of death found in the drawings. It should be pointed out that an external agent may not be required in all cases, since an individual can die from natural causes, from self-directed lethal behaviors, from "being old," and by accident.

The various ways in which death was accomplished were not very well illustrated. This situation did not help to clarify in how many cases an external agent of death may or may not have been called for. The methods that were illustrated included being shot with a gun, being hit by a car, being stabbed by a knife, and

Figure 3–3. Steven (8 years, 4 months): "A man with a knife killed the other man."

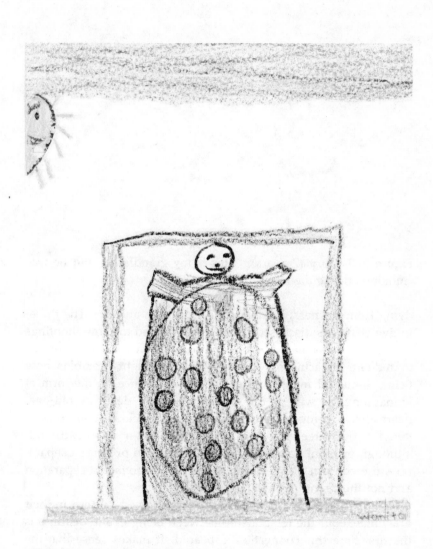

Figure 3–4. Wanita (6 years): "My friend got shot. She is lying on a bed dead."

Figure 3–5. Gary (7 years): "This is my grandfather and he was smoking and he died."

dying from sickness, bombing, electrocution, and fire. The three-to-five year olds discussed in Chapter 2 tended to show shootings and stabbings as methods, but emphasized separation as a primal ingredient for achieving death. The six-to-eight year olds now being discussed mentioned separation only once, in the form of kidnapping, as well as one instance each of death by old age, heart attack, being scared, smoking, loss of blood, and crucifixion. For the three-to-five year olds, separation was death and, although external agents have been needed to produce a separation, the concern of the children was about the fact of separation and not the agent involved.

Although only one boy and two girls showed concern in their drawings about the relationship between being ill and death, it is the first time this connection appeared. It makes sense that the child in the middle years should demonstrate this type of concern, since he is learning to cope with feelings of the self. Included in his lessons is the awareness of the potential for the destruction of that self; "being sick" is one method by which this process can be carried out, possibly ending in death.

The Major Themes Expressed in the Drawings

Six-to-eight year olds showed through their drawings of caskets, crosses, and tombstones, a heightened concern for the ceremonies associated with the dead. The hospital and jail were drawn less frequently but are, nonetheless, clues to the associations children were developing between hospitalization and life and death, as well as with imprisonment as punishment for violent acts. As previously discussed, there was confusion shown by children aged three through eight about the interchangeability of "death" with "the dead." It is uncertain whether this confusion was a function of an imposed adult perspective or if the children actually were confused about these things. Six-through-eight year olds also were confused about the role of the hospital: they showed that the dead were taken there in order to recover to life.

The interests shown by these children in the rites of burial contrast with those interests shown by the three-to-five year olds. The latter are concerned about how people live under changed conditions and ask such questions as "Do dead people eat chocolate cake?," "What is it like living in the cemetary?," and "How does one remove the dirt from one's eyelids and stand up to become alive on earth again?" The younger children do not need to be concerned about burial rites, for the dead are the living. Death is a temporary state of affairs. The older children are losing this viewpoint and replacing it with a growing interest in the rituals of passage out of life.

In addition to showing their interests in the rites of burial, these children also maintained interests in life through the use of such symbols as the sun, clouds, the sky, grass, flowers, and trees. The three-to-five year olds did not incorporate these or other like symbols into their drawings, and neither group of children expressed their feeling about life through water symbols such as streams and rivers.

Figure 3–6. Todd (8 years, 4 months): "A coffin. A person died and was put in a little room because he had no room to bury them. It was in a hill with candles and a cross."

Figure 3–7. Michelle (6 years): "This is at my grandmother's funeral."

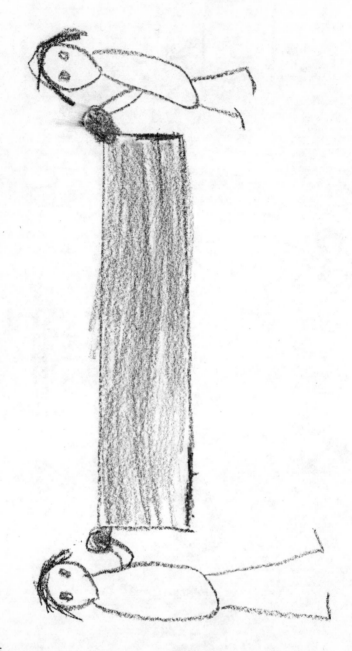

116

Figure 3–8.

It may be said that the features of the drawings of six, seven, and eight year olds are in keeping with the results of Anthony and Nagy, in spite of methodological differences.

Walking is the active characteristic most frequently registered in the drawings, while standing about or lying in beds and in caskets are the most passive characteristics.

A point that has been overlooked in the responses of children and adults to death is the degree of physical contact between the living and the dead. In the drawings we have seen so far, no child showed death or the dead in actual contact with the living. Can we conclude from this finding that death personifications carry with them the message that there is a separation, a distinction between the living and the dead? These representations imply a diminishing, if not complete, loss of a perspective holding to the harmonious and cyclical nature of life and death.

Children's Responses to the Question, "What Happens to People when They Die?"

Children from six to eight years old commented that when people die they get buried and can't move, talk, breathe, see, or eat. Included in these comments are the beginnings of thoughts about the terminality of death. For some children, death can mean the end of life on earth. The dead are limited in their mobility and are seen by an increasing number of children as capable of being transformed into spiritual beings and reaching heaven. These conceptions are consistent with the literature discussed in this chapter.

These children stated that only the "old" are capable of dying. There was no mention of the young succumbing to death; however, pets and specific individuals can and do die, and the young do die in drawings of death. This is important, as such notations indicate the effects of experiences with death or the child's shifting conceptual views of death. This shift is seen here to appear with the beginnings of feelings of terminality, which we will see more frequently with older children.

Some of the concerns shown by six-to-eight year olds are similar to those shown by the younger children—for example, burial, mobility, or aging— but the older children seem to have lost their earlier cosmological view of life and death. For these children, death seems less likely to be an essential part of human existence and the dead have less of a chance of living again. Death for three-to-eight year olds is still associated with the general inability to move out of a restricted environment and to sense the world known by the living. The dead can live and die, again and again, for the three, four, and five year old; but for the older child the dead can be denied a return to life. To further this contrast, the younger child shows minimal interest in life after death. Why should he, since life and death are interchangeable? The older child begins to lose this view in favor of a concern about life after death and of the possible terminal qualities of death.

Some Representative Written Responses Made by Children Aged Six to Eight to the Question, "What Happens to People when They Die?"

Age	Sex	Response
6	M	"Old people get buried and their spirit goes to heaven." "When you die you get buried and don't come back anymore." "When you're very old you die because your body stuff stops working because your bones break."
6	M	"Bodies get buried in the cemetery." "Body stays under the ground." "Bodies can't hear or feel, they just lay . . . but I'm like that when I sleep at night." "The spirit, soul goes to heaven."
6	M	"People go to heaven when they die." "Body goes to heaven and becomes an angel."
6	F	"People die when they go to the hospital."
6	F	"They get old, sick and they get buried." "When you're dead, you can't move or talk, you can't breathe either.
8	M	"When my pet died I felt sad because he did not have enough food. People that die can't see or hear. People that die have to be buried. People that are buried can't do things that living people can do. Soon everyone will die."

8	F	"Your spirit rises up to heaven and their bones stay in the coffin and the angels take the spirit up to heaven. But when you're dead you can't hear, eat, talk or feel. And when you're dead the priest says a prayer and when he finishes the coffin goes in the ground. When people die that is the end of life. When I die the Angel will take my spirit to heaven. I think of death sometimes. One night I had a dream and I screamed in the night when my mother died on the road."
8	F	"When my pet died I felt sad. When people get ready to beie [die] they get buried. Dead people can't feed, the body can't move. Can't talk. Everybody will die [correctly spelled] sometime. My gramma and dad died. Death is final and your heart stops beating."
8	F	"I feel sad. Your spirit goes to heven, if someone died and someone called he or she would not answer. When people die they go to a grave. They cannot touch, think or hear. I think about it in nightmares."
8	F	"I feel sad. My brother had a turtle and it died because it didn't go to sleep in time. It didn't move, it could not hear and its body was very cold and I couldn't hear its hart. My gret gret Grandfather died to. [Actual experience can accelerate development of death conceptions toward the adult view.] When people die it is the end of life. When I die I will be put in a coffin and be buried."
8	F	"Death makes me feel very sad. People that are dead can not feel, hear or touch anything. The dead person goes into the coffin which other people bury it. When any person dies that is the end of their life. When I die that will be the end of my life."
8	M	"When my pet died I felt sorry for him. Because he was only a kitten. When my mom buried him he might be turned into bones. When people die they just turn into bones too. When you die you cannot talk, see, write or anything like that. When you die they bury you in a little yard. I think everybody will die."
8	M	"When a person dies it goes to heaven or hell. Sadness comes to people when someone dies. When something dies it dies of sickness or old age. When they die they go to heaven and start a new life again in heaven. If you are bad most of your life, you will go to hell. Most of us go to heaven. When I think of death I think of sadness."

Table 3–2
Frequency of Responses Given by Children Aged Six Through
Eight to Questions about Death

	Boys		Girls	
	No	*Yes*	*No*	*Yes*
1. Do you ever think about death?	8	16	8	24
2. Does everyone die?	1	23	4	28
3. Will you die someday?	4	20	6	26

Six-to-eight year olds show less confusion about death than the three-to-five year olds (see the appendix to Chapter 2) and have come to believe that everyone will die. They remain a bit less certain whether they will die. The "No" responses recorded in Table 3–2 were given only by six and seven year olds; the eight year olds all gave "Yes" responses to the questions asked.

Children in their middle years are at the threshold of accepting the mortality of others and of themselves. This is consistent with their concerns about their place in the world.

Conclusions

The archetypes of death can be found in the symbols associated with the dark, emptiness, formlessness, water, sleep, rebirth, and personifications. In children's fantasies, death is characteristically described as a bringer of sorrow and fear or a separater of child from parent or of parents from each other. In such fantasies, figures can move between life and death or between distinct physical modalities (from corpse to ghost), and can become involved in aggressive or punishing activities such as kidnapping, shooting, stabbing, hitting, and scaring. In the present sample of children, personifications are apparent but the specific agents of death or separation are not as frequently described as might have been expected, and seem to be replaced by an increased concern over the rituals of burial.

A listing of symbols and activities concerned with death was one of the results of Hite's (1968) analysis of her adult patients. Some of the entries in this list were burning in a fire, swimming, drowning, holding onto a ring, sex, hunger, the color of green, children playing, plants, and birds struggling. It has been proposed that the symbolization of traumatic or threatening events is a way of integrating that is curative (Kelman, 1960). This line of reasoning can be thought to include the drawings and personifications of children, for their drawings are meaningful symbolic messages and not merely representations of worldly phenomena.

There are, however, questions that beg for answers. Is it a good thing to personify death? Is it healthy to show an early interest in burial rites?

There is little evidence in the psychological literature to draw from, but what does find its way into print suggests, for example, that personifications of death as being male or female are positively related to greater anxiety about death than personifications of a nonsexual nature. That is, male and female adults who saw death as being a sexless presence expressed consistently less anxiety about death (Lonetto et al., 1976). On a larger scale, Aries (1962) has noted that the more Western society liberated itself from Victorian views of sexuality, the more it rejected death. Interestingly, the combination of eroticism and death has reappeared in our passion for sadistic and violent literature.

Childhood concerns with burial rites have been taboo for the social sciences, so the best we can do is extrapolate from the studies done on adults.

The children's drawings reveal their use of personification to deal with death and the rites associated with the dead. For a few children this includes the hospital. These aspects of children's drawings represent the many faces of reality; in particular, their personifications are essential means for relating their conceptualizations, since personification can transcend ordinary language.

At least some, and perhaps many, readers want to know what kinds of data we are talking about. This question typically is asked because the ideal of our science has been to obtain an objective world view without the interference of a human observer. We act as if our science could produce information, the validity of which is absolute. This is our problem, and it reflects in our approach to the mysteries of the universe. At one time, Newton's laws of nature and mechanics were considered to be the ultimate explanations of natural phenomena. Less than 100 years later, physicists experimenting with the world of atoms made the limitations of the Newtonian model both visible and empirical. Modern physicists revealed the basic oneness of the universe and showed that we cannot decompose the world into its smallest irreducible units.

We have to be aware of "the observer," for events and phenomena can be understood only in terms of their interactions with this observer. This is the case for our conceptions of death. We would like to treat these conceptual systems as independent of human intervention, but they are not.

If personifications and the rites of burial achieve a separation of the living from the dead, they are processes that take apart the unity of the world that the younger child understood and took for a given. These notions can now separate the older child from the world. The child may indeed separate and be faced with seeing life and death as beginning and end points in a continuum. Both the young child and the modern physicist see the inseparability of phenomena. The more mature child is pulling the world apart and changing circularity into oscillatory movements where the birth to death continuum signals a break, an emptiness, an unknown. The child is caught up in the importance of beginnings and endings in a search for causal explanations. This eventually will lead him to forget completely the harmonious cycle of life and death. The younger child has no need for such thoughts, for in a world of circles there are no beginnings or endings. He has no use for causal models.

Appendix to Chapter 3

Summary of the Contents of the Drawings of Children Aged Six through Eight: Frequency of Responses

Response Type	Males (n = 25)	Females (n = 34)
Colors used		
Black	22	25
Red	17	25
Yellow	12	18
Brown	18	20
Purple	7	16
Orange	11	21
Blue	13	21
Green	13	21
Number of colors used		
1	3	4
2	3	3
3	4	3
4	5	2

Response Type	Males (n = 25)	Females (n = 34)
5	3	3
6	9	19
Physical features		
None	2	3
Hair	11	27
Ears	4	1
Eyebrows	1	1
Eyes: two	23	31
more than two	0	0
Eyelashes	1	3
Nose	19	27
Mouth: smiling	13	17
frowning/in pain	6	9
open	4	2
Neck	7	15
Body: yes	23	27
no	0	2
Navel	1	0
Arms: two	22	29
more than two	1	0
Hands: with fingers	11	7
without fingers	2	2
Legs: two	22	28
more than two	1	0
Feet: two	14	11
more than two	0	0
Gender		
Male	17	20
Female	3	5
Unspecified	3	6
Nonhuman form	3	2
Age		
Infant	0	0
Child	4	8
Adult	5	5
Aged (e.g., grandparent)	1	8
Undetermined	14	18
Actions		
None	1	0
Walking	4	5
Talking	0	1
Watching	3	3
Eyes closed	0	0

Response Type	Males (n = 25)	Females (n = 34)
Smelling	0	0
Sneezing	0	0
Touching	0	0
Standing	15	12
Lying down: in bed	8	11
because of fatigue	0	0
Running	1	1
Hiding	1	1
Digging in the ground	1	0
Funeral services	4	5
Calling for help	0	1
Specific contents		
A blob	1	2
Articles in house	0	1
Bed	0	2
Birds	1	1
Blood	5	3
Bomb	1	0
Buildings (nonspecific)	0	1
Candles	1	0
Casket	8	10
Clouds	3	3
Cross	2	4
Dirt	3	3
Dog	0	0
Electric outlet	1	0
Flowers	2	5
Fork	0	1
Glasses	2	0
Grass	9	11
Gun	5	2
Hats	2	1
Hearse	0	0
Hearts and tears	0	1
Horse	0	0
House	1	6
Hospital	0	1
Insect (e.g., bee)	1	1
Knife	2	2
Mask	1	0
Monster	4	1
Mountain	0	0
Orange sucker	0	0
Parachute	0	0

Response Type	Males (n = 25)	Females (n = 34)
Plane	0	0
Policeman	0	1
Rain	0	0
Shovel	2	0
Sky	5	5
Snake	0	1
Snow	0	0
Squirrel	1	0
Stars	0	0
Sun	9	5
TV	0	0
Tank	1	0
Thunder	0	0
Tombstone	3	8
Trees	2	4
Vehicles (cars, ambulances)	0	2
Water	0	0
Windows/doors	2	8
Actions associated with death		
Attacked by a monster	0	1
Attacked by snakes	0	1
Being buried: in the ground	4	8
in a box	5	3
Being scared	2	0
Being separated	0	2
Being sick (e.g., heart attack)	2	2
Bleeding	3	2
Blood sucking (e.g., by a vampire)	1	0
Bombing/war	3	1
Car accident	1	1
Crucifixion	0	1
Electrocution	1	1
Fire	0	3
Hitting	0	0
Hurting	1	0
Kidnapping	0	1
Shooting	6	4
Smoking	1	0
Stabbing	2	2
Not described	9	18

The reader should note that more than one method associated with the death of figure(s) in the children's drawings may be found in each drawing.

Who Was Killed and by Whom:

	Sex of Person Killed			
Sex of Killer	*Male*	*Female*	*?*	*Death*
Male	13	4	10	2
Female	15	13	11	
?	8	17		
Death				

4

The Child from Nine through Twelve Years

The Child in Transition

The period of growth between 9 and 12 years of age has not been given the attention that has been bestowed upon earlier and later periods of development. This is of some interest, as children in this age range begin to initiate separations from the family while attaching themselves to their peer groups. It is also a time when children are able to perceive their parents as being less than perfect in terms of their judgments or standards.

The social sciences have tended to think of this age range as merely a transitory phase with its basic importance to be found in its overlap with the onset of adolescence. This approach is to be expected, as children have been examined in relation to their maturity based upon adult models; therefore, adolescence, having closer proximity to the realm of the adult, gathers a larger share of research efforts and reports. To bypass 9-to-12 year olds is to diminish the drama of the leaving of childhood. At this point, the child is standing in a kind of preadolescent limbo that implies both a reaching back toward early days and a reaching toward the future. Psychologists and sociologists concerned about the developing child do appear to agree that the basic tasks associated with 9-to-12 year olds are:

1. To gain a sense of the self outside of the family
2. To understand the rules of society in order to find a place in the world of peers
3. To continue the developmental pattern of learning about oneself in the world.

Reports on the physical growth of children from 9 to 12 years of age indicate that they experience, on the average, a rather steady growth and are relatively free from the diseases that were a common feature of their early childhood. This period of growth also can become emeshed, of course, with feelings of awkwardness and consciousness about the self, especially if such growth is beyond the bounds of what is considered to be normal (Strang, 1959). The boundaries for acceptable growth seem to be for 9-year-old boys to attain a weight of 66 pounds and a height of 53.3 inches. This should increase, on the average, to a weight of 84.4 pounds and a height of 58.9 inches at 12 years. Nine-year-old girls stand about 52.3 inches and carry around 63.8 pounds. At 12 years, their average weight should be 87.6 pounds with a height of 59.8 inches. The boys will have to wait until the age of 14 to stand taller and weigh more than the average girl.

All of this good health and growth may serve as a prerequisite condition for the child to be in a position to survive the physical and mental adjustments of preadolescence and adolescence, including the appearance of acne, puberty, and permanent teeth. The onset of puberty can be seen in 10-year-old girls and 12-year-old boys, but it is more usual not to notice these indicators until girls are 12 years old and boys are 14 years old.

The healthy growing period for 9-to-12 year olds also shapes the awakening of thoughts and feelings about sexual matters. This is apparent in the emotional identifications with one's own sex group, in selecting the first brassiere, and in play. The play activities of 9-to-12 year olds help the child to deal with fears about sexuality in much the same way as play aided younger children to deal with their fears about death. These activities certainly suggest that peer groups provide for children a basic teaching program about life. There has been abundant discussion and speculation about just how much children learn about sex from their peers, as compared to how much they learn from their parents. Unfortunately, there is a lack of such discussion when the question is raised as to how much children learn about death from their peers, rather than from their parents.

The full impact of peer group socialization rituals, either on the child or on his movement into adulthood, is still not fully understood. Documentation does exist concerning the child's desire to be with peers, to appear competent to peers, and to gain their approval (Gesell, Ilg, and Ames, 1956; Kanous, Daugherty, and Cohn, 1962; Hurlock, 1968). These components of peer group influence generally are observed, along with the increasing loyalty the child feels towards peers. This attachment to his peer group adds to the child's confidence as he questions and rejects some of the standards of adults.

Two often-noted effects of peer group identification on the development of the child are (1) the separation of sexes in play activities and, related to this, (2) the establishment of "secret" clubs. The preference that 9-to-12 year olds show for being in the company of others similar to themselves also can be found in adults (Schachter, 1959; Wheeler, 1970). In the search for his "self," the child demonstrates a clear need for the presence of, and contact with, peers who are perceived to be similar.

The more complete the absorption of the child into the peer group, the more the child perceives that parents, and other adults, can make mistakes. The once-perfect rulers now are not so powerfully autocratic. They are weakened by misjudgments, faulty arguments, and inconsistent actions; and can be questioned directly and even rejected as the sole guide for how one's life should be conducted and rewarded. This procedural change in the child's dealings with adults is intended to lead to emotional stability and security. Such a position orientation is a welcome surprise, as the social sciences have not presented what could be said to be an optimistic view of humankind. In this instance, there is almost no mention of the potentially disturbing effects of this altered perspective of adults. The possibility exists that the questioning and rejection of adult standards could make the child feel doubtful and fearful about growing up.

Piaget (1932) has suggested that children may see their parents as unable to change and as being old, and thus may alter their views about their parents' authority over them and in the world. Concepts of parents shift toward specifics and do not become expanded generalities. The awesome powers parents exercised in earlier times over forces in the world are diminished, and continue to do so as the child matures. This is an important phase in the child's development of conceptions about the nature of his interactions with others in the world. As the child pulls back from the family, perceptions of the father may change. The father can be seen as a link to the outside world, an independent agent to be trusted or held in suspicion.

The child's movement, away from the family and toward peers, brings along with it the terrible burden of having to be popular. Now the polarities of growing up become apparent as the child learns that part of what he calls "himself" is a reflection of how he is seen by others. He can choose to limit the scope of these reflections and their influences on him, or yield to them. The nature of the child's interactions with others affects the ease with which he can develop a personality that matches his concerns about the world he lives in. A child may find that schoolmates make him different than he is at home, and different from what he thought he was. He may feel that, as Jung (1977, pp. 49–50) noted, he is at least two different persons: sometimes a schoolboy; at other times an important, respected figure not to be fooled about with.

Play becomes a way to venture into the fantasies of childhood and test out notions about reality. The activities of 9-to-12 year olds have been described as "I dare you" and "follow the leader";

both are paths for the attainment of peer approval, either for being brave and daring or for going along with others. The child seems to be developing a part of his conscious awareness of the self-in-the-world that is concerned with needs for approval and how to satisfy these needs.

As if the forgoing situations weren't enough for 9-to-12 year olds to cope with, these children are thought to be anxious and to display a number of fears. These can take the forms of distrust and withdrawal from parents, as well as increased fears about the supernatural. School is felt to be their most common source of worry and frustration. Other specific anxieties include their health and the health of parents, being in dark or high places, being around strange animals, being alone, and the possibility of being called "chicken" (Hurlock,1968).

It is not unlikely that the anxieties of 9-to-12 year olds could cause them to turn to spiritual and ethical explanations as ways of coping. The position taken by the research literature is that these children are developing relative standards about moral issues, but are too immature to experience insights of a more profound spiritual nature (Britton and Winaus, 1958). The 9 year old is said to lack strong religious interests, whereas the 10 year old is believed to see God as an invisible man, and the 11 or 12 year old is thought to see God as a spiritual being.

At the age of 11, Jung (1977) recalled that the idea of God held some interest for him. This was a God who was a "very powerful, old man" who could gain his trust. It is an image containing the major contradiction of the twentieth century: to be old and very powerful. Old age in our culture usually is accompanied by weakness and helplessness, not by increased powers.

The 9-to-12 year old still remains within the confines of cognitive and moral development as drawn by Piaget. He is said to be at the concrete operational stage and moving toward abstract thinking that is contaminated at least to some degree by social approval. He is able to make decisions and utilize information presented to him in making judgments about events around him. The shift toward abstract thought is, in part, triggered by the child's awareness of relative standards, of other viewpoints, of differences of opinion. Children become fascinated with intervening variables while discovering how to employ social languages at school (the sciences and humanities) and slang with their peers. Although these language systems seldom, if ever, provide genuine insights, they do provide the child with a storehouse of knowledge to help him communicate with others who have acquired similar information.

In Piagetian terms (1932), the child of 9 to 12 years is incapable of formal, logical thought. This must be all the more frustrating for their teachers and parents, as children are full of questions about the physical world and about growing up. The child is able to link time and space and can project back into the past and on into the future as he extends and tests out his sense of self. He is attempting to find a continuum to take him into the emerging world of adolescence. The 9-to-12 year old has left the eternal time of early childhood and is now faced with a time that continues to move out before him, a time that seems to pass.

Children's Concepts of Death: Ages Nine through Twelve

The oldest children In Nagy's (1948) study realized that death (1) marks the cessation of corporeal life (finality) and (2) is a process operating within each of us (internality and universality). These responses are in contrast to the descriptions of death as externalized (through personifications) by 5-to-9 year olds. Death for the 9-to-12 year old has become inevitable. No one escapes or recovers from death.

The work of Childers and Wimmer (1971) and Steiner (1965) supports the view of the child's gradually increasing awareness of the universality of death. There is less unequivocal support for the notion that this awareness also embraces the irrevocability of death; this seems to be less consistently associated with the age of the child. Kastenbaum and Aisenberg (1972) further suggest that children from 9 to 12 years of age may not differ from adolescents in the "content" of their death conceptions; the major difference may lie in the "significance" these concerns have for their total cognitive development.

Results derived from retrospective questionaires (Scott, 1896; Hall, 1922; Caprio, 1950), interviews (Anthony, 1940; Nagy, 1948), observations of play (Rochlin, 1967), and controlled experiments (Alexander and Adlerstein, 1958) are in some agreement that the child's conception of death moves from a state of nonawareness (denial), through an intermediate stage where death is external-ized in many forms (the skeleton-man, ghosts, and the like), to one of an appreciation of death as universal. The caution here is that this agreement is restricted to the description of developmen-tal stages of attitudes toward death. There still is considerable disagreement in terms of explanations for the characteristic re-sponses at specific age and maturational levels. The findings of Childers and Wimmer (1971) are illustrative of this situation; they reported that, although no strong pattern emerged in the devel-opment of the child's beliefs about death, the age of 9 years is a kind of cognitive turning point at which death is seen as being universal. A similar argument was not made, however, for the child perceiveing death as irrevocable.

In the research literature concerned with the child's gaining an awareness of death, there is the implicit statement that a certain amount of immaturity is attached to the inability to ac-cept the inevitability of death. Denial is considered to be a most immature response to death and very much associated with a lack of proper emotional development. Denial has become re-served for those of us who possess fragile egos that would surely shatter with the knowledge that death cannot really be "denied." In order for the child to gain a foothold in the adult world, he has to learn to accept the finality of death, and reject his earliest cyclical conceptions.

The progression of conceptions about death might be described in a more generalized way by stating that such combinations of thoughts and attitudes include supernatural and biological determinants, both of which can be replaced with symbolic determinants. It does seem that the 9-to-12 year old's view of death (that is, of the biological failure of organs to function, thus causing or hastening death) stays with him throughout adolescence and into later life. Very few of us have taken the time to re-examine in depth "what death is and means" after we have passed through the stage of biological determinism. As adults, we tend to favor empiricism over conceptualization and, therefore, we have spent our efforts studying the biological side of death, while spending considerably less effort in examining other possible and perhaps more profoundly human factors. The stress we have put upon biological explanations and causation may be a way for us to avoid coping with the anxieties of our children. One common rationale for the amount of time spent on empirical pursuits is the assumption that if we give children good, hard, scientific evidence for death, then we have taught them enough. Prior to the emergence of this biological perspective, the position taken in the literature was that children do not understand what death is all about, and so we do not need to deal with their anxieties about it. When they reach the level of understanding of the biological factors associated with death, then their anxieties will diminish with this knowledge, for the knowledge of science, of facts, should free the mind. If this were the case, then 9-to-12 year olds should exhibit less anxiety about death than younger or even older children.

The research of Alexander and Adlerstein (1958) usually is offered to confirm that the period between 9 and 12 years is one of benign latency, a period in which no new demands are made of the child nor are new response alternatives called for. In their study, the 5-to-8 year olds and the 13-to-16 year olds showed decreased skin resistance (increased anxiety), as measured by GSRs (galvanic skin responses) to death-related words; while the effect was minimized for the 9-to-12 year olds. It was felt that these findings were associated with the relative stability of ego functioning for each age group, with the 9-to-12 year olds thus demonstrating the most stable functioning.

In another empirically oriented study, Ross (1967) attempted to assess the relationships in 9 year olds between separation anxiety, fear of death, and fear of strangers. The results of the work indicated that separation and death fears were linked in a dynamic way, and that this relationship was especially potent for first-born children.

If the GSR realistically can be considered a direct measure of anxiety, then results using such less direct methods as interviews, observations, drawings, and other projective techniques generally have shown that 9-to-12 year olds are concerned about death and about being dead (Nagy, 1948; Anthony, 1973; Childers and Wimmer, 1971; Rochlin, 1967). Conflicting outcomes are frequent in studies of anxiety and fears about death, which seems to be due to the diversity of methodologies used, including sampling procedures and analytic strategies. The interested reader is directed to Lonetto, Fleming, and Mercer (1979) for a more detailed discussion of these issues.

In spite of the so-called benign latency of these children, one feels uneasy that they can be so calm about death, especially when one considers that it is during this phase in their development that they reduce their animistic-magical interpretations in favor of biological ones. These render death inevitable, universal, and, more often than not, final. This package of beliefs about mortality should carry with it at least some anxiety, for now the child begins to realize that *he can die* as well. Alexander and Adlerstein have tried to simplify the complex cognitive structures of children to fit the movements of GSR recordings, while leaving aside the problems of "why children from 9 to 12 years of age should *not* feel anxiety about the inevitability and finality of death."

In Nagy's study, children of about 9 or 10 saw death as a lawful process that takes place in each of us. Children past the age of 9 years in Anthony's study could give general, logical, and biologically "correct" responses when asked to give definitions of the word "dead." These conceptions of death are thought to reflect the child's changing view of himself in the world. It is a world where destruction can take place from within. The importance of this stage in the development of conceptions about death is that mortality becomes a personal affair, for the child now realizes he can die. Now that death has achieved this universal and personal status, the child may show an interest in questions about the afterlife and what happens to dead bodies. Anthony has noted that children 9 years of age and older would rather perform a ceremonial burial of a dead animal, to ensure its passage into the afterlife, than dissect it to see how it works, as they might have preferred at an earlier stage in their development.

Safier's (1964) interviews with 30 boys aged 4 to 10 years demonstrated a shift from outside agents of death being of dominant concern, for children younger than 10 years, to the principle of internal causes at about 10 years. Kane's (1975) work not only demonstrated that death comes from within for 12 year olds, but that it also renders the person unable to feel. This is a shift from seeing life and death as given and taken away by powerful and mysterious outside forces, to a position emphasizing that life and death are somehow capable of being determined by internal forces. This shift, however, is by no means absolute, as personifications of death can still be found. Peter, aged 9 years 11 months, felt that death could come and carry you off (Safier, 1964). In fact, death could carry everyone off. Death is dangerous, invisible at times, skeleton-like, and can disappear like a vampire with the morning light. For boys and girls of about 10 years of age, death could be a spirit or a ghost.

If we believe that the presence of death is a motive behind all forms of human activity, then what happens to the child who comes to believe that death is universal and inevitable? Will the child feel, as adults have felt, that if he is going to die anyway, what's the use? The age range of 9 to 12 years has been characterized as a time of benign development, but there are still some demons lurking about.

Maurer's (1964) work with adolescents' attitudes toward death bears directly on these issues, for she attempted to relate considerations of death with achievement—in this case, academic success. Her hypothesizing such a relationship is understandable within our cultural framework. To her credit, she does point out that anxiety about death is a component of one's emotional maturity, as well as one's defenses against this form of anxiety.

Students were asked to respond to the following questions: (1) What comes to your mind when you think of death? and (2) What comes to your mind when you think of love? The second question was added to reduce the traumatic effect of the first. Maurer stated that this second question was a necessary addition because the first one alone would immobilize the students, and they would be unable to respond. It is rather difficult to believe that "love" is not traumatic for adolescents, in view of their songs, literature, and neurotic concerns about it. The descriptions given by Maurer of the testing situation are all the more enlightening: the students were enrolled in a class called "Healthy Family Living."

Of more concern for our 9-to-12 year olds are the statements made by 17-to-19 year olds about death. They were filled with references to sadness, remorse, loneliness, and uncertainty. Their responses were more elaborate than those given by 9-to-12 year olds, but the point remains that they still were quite similar (See Nagy, 1948; Anthony, 1973; and the section to follow on Children's Drawings of Death.) The adolescents' responses contained references to peace, beauty, distaste for the dead, the smells of funerals, and the occurrence of accidents and murder. The responses given by Maurer's subjects also contained personifications of death, but with the absence of denial. Death clearly was seen to be the end of life.

Two statements in particular show the overlap of concerns adolescents share with 9-to-12 year olds, as well as the effects of socialization on the child's view of death. The statements were: "I am scared to death of death" and "I am so embarrassed that I could die." In the latter statement it should be pointed out that embarrassment of this sort can happen only to the child whose "I" has been properly socialized.

This study concluded that the fear of death and the inevitability of death are related, though not very strongly, to achievement. Those with less ability show more fear. Maurer does not go on to question and interpret these relationships in any depth. Questions remain as to what human-social values should be placed on these relationships; or whether school teaches fear, especially to those who cannot demonstrate specific academic skills. Maurer also failed to follow up on Kastenbaum's (1977) observations that adolescents put as much time as possible between themselves and death.

Thirty-five children of a mean age of 10.4 years responded to Koocher's (1973) question "when will you die?" by saying that death would occur at 81.3 years (standard deviation = 12.68 years), while 20 children of a mean age of 13.3 years felt that 81.4 years (standard deviation = 9.54 years) was the appropriate time for death. None of the children in the study who were older than nine years thought that it was possible to bring the dead back to life. Death happens to the aged and death is final. These children also were concerned about what would happen after they died. Fifty-two percent talked about burial, 21% about the afterlife, 19% about funerals, 3% about cremation, and 10% had no idea what would happen. These response percentages were not presented by Koocher by specific age grouping or by sex.

Although the evidence is skimpy at best, it does appear, in general, that 9-to-12 year olds see death as being associated with the aged and, of course, they have quite a few years to live before death overtakes them—about 70 years.

Does the universality of death include within its boundaries the notion of taking one's life? Adults generally believe that childhood suicide is not possible and that threats to commit the act are, for the most part, gestures to gain attention. But what of the 9-to-12 year old who is beginning to see death in adultlike terms? Can a child in this age range commit suicide?

> 'Fritz, aged 10, closed the kitchen door and turned on the gas oven, to make his mother nervous like his father does' . . . Rosa, aged 11, lived in a home where there was constant quarrelling. 'She went to the roof of their apartment house whenever arguments . . . began. For a while, the family would follow her, when they stopped, she began to stand on the roof edge. Finally she jumped and suffered multiple injuries.'
>
> (Yochelson, 1967, p. 99)

Some of the factors that are thought to precipitate suicidal behaviors are (1) preoccupation with death to the extent that children want to see their parents overcome with grief and sorrow for treating them so badly, (2) parental neglect, (3) constant moving from one home to another without sufficient explanations by parents for these moves, (4) parental pressures to succeed, especially in school, (5) periods of illness, and (6) lack of close friendships. In short, a range of factors is responsible, none of which taken singularly can account for the majority of the self-destructive behaviors of children.

The point here is that adults are hampered in their arguments against childhood suicide when it comes to 9-to-12 year olds because these children are aware of death in biological and universal terms. They manifest a maturity of concepts similar to those held by adults.

Children's Drawings of Death: Ages Nine through Twelve

Nine Year Olds

There are still fragments of confusion of the dead with death, as found in the drawings of younger children, particularly when the dead included family members; however, grandparents are seen to die more frequently than fathers, uncles, or aunts. As yet, no child showed his mother to be one of the dead. These children also show concern in their drawings over the death of animals (dogs, cats, skunks, and birds) and of all the dead people they do not know. A most important result of this drawing exercise is that 4 of the 18 children could perceive their own death as inevitable but not in the immediate future, for such a death could occur only when they were old.

Concern about the methods of death were present in the drawings and involved shooting and/or stabbing, accidents (car crashes), illness (heart attacks) and old age. Only one child illustrated that death could be accompanied by the act of killing oneself; in all other depictions of death, some form of external agent was required.

The children were interested in the condition of the dead, who were seen as turning to dust; as not being able to hear, talk, see or move; and as being happy, to list a few of their descriptions. Children reacted to death with sadness (n = 12), a feeling that death was bad (n = 6), and a feeling of fear (n = 3). The rituals associated with burying the dead were shown by 13 children and, for the first time, cremation appeared as a method for treating the dead (n = 2).

Children showed concern in their drawings about both personification of death and the ceremonies of burial. Along with these features are found depictions of a number of methods for achieving death, but the external agent utilizing these methods very often is not included. Their drawings reflect more of the life symbols that were absent in the drawings of the younger children, such as the sky, grass, the sun, and flowers. The water symbol has not yet made its appearance.

These responses are a function of the children's ability to incorporate their experiences with death into both their drawings and their discussions of the drawings. They show more concern than younger children about what happens to the dead; the relationship between illness, old age, and death; and specific experiences with death, such as the death of a family member or of an animal. The children now are expressing their feelings for those who have died and will die, and some children included themselves in this latter group.

Ten Year Olds

These children tend to see death as a horrible, terrible thing, whether it be the death of others or their own death. The place of death is full of darkness and gloom. Their concerns are more with the scary features of death than with the rites of burial and the methods for achieving death, save for their fears about being murdered or dying a painful death. Death of the child himself

Figure 4–1. Victor (9 years, 4 months): "A man died. People came to read the brick. There is blood all over. A man shoot him. He doesn't know he is in the coffin."

Figure 4–2. Tammy (8 years, 8 months): "A man is stabbing another man on a bed. They will put him in a coffin and bury him. He may go to heaven or the devil."

Figure 4–3. Terry Lynne (8 years, 8 months): "I drew a coffin with x's and o's and love all over it."

now becomes more centralized than the possible or real death of others.

In their discussions of their drawings, the children made many references to the "fact" that everyone has to die, including themselves. Many discussed their concern with life after death. They wanted to know what death was like. Some children wished that someone would come back from the dead to tell them all about what it is like to die, even if other people thought they were crazy. Only two children felt that death is a joyous event, that the ultimate life is in heaven. This is in contrast to the fears of the other children about what happens after death.

The happy smiles of the dead depicted by the younger children have all but faded away in the representations given by 10 year olds, who show the dead with closed mouths and eyes.

Personification of death and the ceremonials of the dead exist in these drawings but contain more adult-oriented elements than the drawings completed by younger children. In the drawings of 10 year olds there is sadness and tears; there is horror in the killing of a girl by a man and in an animal lying bloodied after being hit by a car. Realism is emerging. The time has come for at least one child's mother to lose her immunity to the approach of death.

Eleven Year Olds

Although there is some interest in personification and burial rituals, it is declining as compared to younger children. There is however, an increasing use of symbols to represent feelings about death and the dead, such as tears, a broken heart, and a tree with its limbs bare of leaves. Symbolic usage at higher levels of abstraction also is found in the drawings of 11 year olds. In these drawings, shapes and forms in spatial arrangements demonstrate what death is. For at least six of these children, death has lost its human or bestial trappings and has become an abstract form.

Their comments about their drawings show that the children have accepted the notion that death is inevitable and cannot be

Figure 4–4. Lisa (10 years).

Figure 4–5. Marnie (10 years).

prevented. Death can take you regardless of age, for now both the very old and the young can die. The children are afraid of death, saddened by it, and want to die in a painless way. These reactions are quite similar to those given by adults when asked to describe the ways in which they think they will die (Sabatini and Kastenbaum, 1973; Lonetto et al., 1975).

The desire for a painless death marks an important turning point in the child's conception of death. Prior to 10 years of age, considerations of pain are absent or minimal, but they grow in importance as the child moves toward the adult viewpoint. The child is gaining an awareness of the mortality of the self, as well as of pain and suffering.

Figure 4–6. Jeff (10 years).

These 11 year olds showed a specific fear of being buried alive, because they believed that they could be eaten by worms or bugs even though they would be in caskets beneath the ground. Cremation was seen by three of the children as a way of avoiding the problem of being eaten while dead.

Twelve Year Olds

Both boys and girls showed a preference for the use of black to represent their feelings about death. For 9 of the 20 boys, black was the only color used, as it was for 5 of the 20 girls. We have not seen the use of one color to this extent since the presentation of the drawings of 3-to-5 year olds.

Eight boys and 7 girls included neither human nor nonhuman features in their drawings of death. When features were drawn,

Death

Means Saddness

Figure 4–7. Kim (11 years).

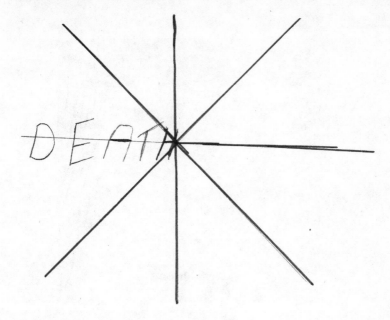

Figure 4–8. Kevin (11 years).

they tended to be somber, slightly evil, or sad. As examples of this turn in perception of death, mouths were set in frowns, were open in fear, or were shown to be sneering at death or the dead. Only two girls created a smiling mouth on the face of death. Boys perceived death as a male figure, while girls saw death as male, female, or in nonsexual nonhuman terms. The age of death or of the dead ranged from childhood through adulthood, but specific age-related descriptions were largely missing from the drawings. Unlike the 9 year olds, these 12 year olds did not represent death or the dead as being aged. In fact, a prominent characteristic of these drawings is the lack of activities performed by agents of death or by others, human or not. Crying, stabbing, standing about, and bleeding were shown in a small number of drawings. (For a complete summary of the contents of these children's drawings, see the appendix to this chapter.)

The specific contents of the drawings that were available for analysis demonstrated the children's concern with the rituals as-

Figure 4–9. Brian (11 years). "Death is Sadness."

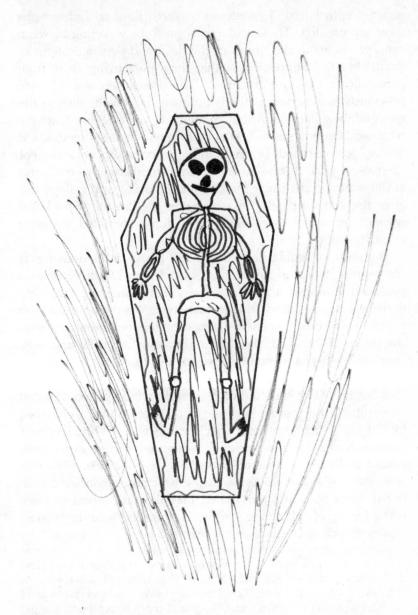

Figure 4–10. Eric (11 years, 11 months).

sociated with burial. Tombstones, caskets, flowers, and wreaths were represented. These children seem to be wavering between conceptions about the rituals of the dead and personifications of death, but the impression is that they are moving away from personification and toward ritual. Their drawings contained some previously unreported methods for achieving death, such as the rack and the guillotine. Although methods for achieving death are recorded, there is still a hesitancy to mention these methods at all, as demonstrated by their infrequency of appearance. For 12-year-old girls, this hesitancy is complete: there was no attempt at illustrating a particular method for achieving death. Boys and girls also have difficulty in noting the specifics of "who killed whom?" In the few cases where the victim is identified, the giver of death is not.

The most intriguing new component found in the drawings is the representation of death in abstract terms. Death becomes a profound darkness, a great blackness that is shown by the children in a page of black crayon markings. We thus can add the perception of death as an abstraction to children's concerns over the rituals of the dead, their personifications of death, and their confusion between personifying death and the dead.

In their comments about death, the children felt that people died because (1) if they didn't, the world would be too crowded (n = 10), (2) they reached old age (n = 9), or (3) they were felled by a disease such as a heart attack or cancer (n = 10). The boys saw death as a horrible, terrifying, scary, and painful experience, similar to the perceptions of 10 year olds. For the girls, death was scary and was seen in terms of the heartbreak associated with burial. Both boys and girls stated that all death meant to them was a feeling of "blackness," which is consistent with the abstract representation of death found in their drawings.

> Death is blackness . . . like when you close your eyes. It's cold and when you die your body is cold. Frightening, I don't want to die . . . I wonder then, how I'm going to die . . . I feel scared and I try to forget it. When I feel like this, I try to forget it and just put something else into my mind.
>
> Jenny, aged 11 years 10 months

Figure 4–11. Jelica (12 years, 3 months). "Brown to represent dirt; Grey ———; Black to represent darkness; Red to represent blood."

The age of 12 years may embody a continuation of the conceptual systems of earlier years, as seen in the children's representations of the rituals of the dead; as well as a transition, as seen in their abstract views of death. In their comments, the children showed some adultlike beliefs about the pain, sorrow, and terror of death, but their drawings and comments did not fixate on biological death.

Figure 4–12. Phillip (12 years, 3 months). "The Mask of Death."

Conclusions

The drawings and comments of 9-to-12 year olds display both uniqueness and common concerns. In terms of the unique elements associated with each age level, we find the 9 year olds show concern over the deaths of particular people, with emphasis upon the deaths of grandparents. These children are able to incorporate their experiences into their interpretations of death; thus, death becomes related to old age, illness, and disease. These children also show an interest in the condition of the dead. The 10 year olds are troubled about the gloom, doom, and pain imposed by death. They are the first group of children to perceive the death of the mother. No other age group seems capable of rendering lifeless such an influential figure in their lives. The deaths of grandparents, however, are acceptable. It may be that an older individual loses the powerful mystique of parenthood for these children. They have lost sight of the fact that these individuals are the parents of their parents. Eleven year olds know that death is inevitable and desire a painless death. Some 12 year olds represent death in abstract terms and show a distinct lack of activity in their drawings of death.

The common concerns shown across the age groups are seen in children's expressed awareness of self-mortality, in their distinct fears of death, in their interests in the rituals of burial, and in their feelings about the inevitability of death. Children from 9 to 12 years old seem capable not only of perceiving death as biological, universal, and inevitable, but of coming to an appreciation of the abstract nature of death and of describing the feelings generated by this quality. This complex recognition pattern associated with death is joined by an emerging belief in the mortality of the self, but for these children death is far in the future and remains in the domain of the aged.

Appendix to Chapter 4

Summary of the Contents of the Drawings of Children Aged Nine through Twelve: Frequency of Responses

Response Type	Males (n = 46)	Females (n = 61)
Colors Used		
Black	34	48
Red	20	41
Yellow	13	31
Brown	24	31
Purple	9	9
Orange	14	16
Blue	18	31
Green	10	30
Number of colors used		
1	12	8
2	4	4
3	7	12
4	4	9

Response Type	Males (n = 46)	Females (n = 61)
5	9	10
6	10	19
Physical Features		
None	15	22
Hair	17	28
Ears	2	2
Eyebrows	1	9
Eyes: two	25	27
more than two	1	0
Eyelashes	0	7
Nose	24	24
Mouth: smiling	3	5
frowning/in pain	21	23
open	3	4
Neck	12	15
Body: yes	22	23
no	3	2
Navel	0	0
Arms: two	20	23
more than two	2	0
Hands: with fingers	11	15
without fingers	9	6
Legs: two	20	17
more than two	1	0
Feet: two	19	17
more than two	1	0
Gender		
Male	13	15
Female	4	16
Unspecified	6	7
Nonhuman form	5	4
Age		
Infant	0	0
Child	6	9
Adult	4	4
Aged (e.g., grandparent)	5	6
Undetermined	19	25
Actions		
Bleeding	8	2
Calling for help	3	0
Crying	6	16
Digging in the ground/buried	4	3
Eyes closed	0	0

Response Type	Males (n = 46)	Females (n = 61)
Flying	1	2
Funeral services	0	0
Hiding	0	0
Lying down: in bed	0	4
on ground	1	3
because of fatigue	0	0
in casket	6	2
None	11	14
Praying	0	3
Running	0	0
Smelling	0	0
Sneezing	0	0
Standing	11	11
Talking	0	0
Touching	0	0
Walking	4	4
Watching	5	4
Specific contents		
A blob	5	4
Angel	0	1
Articles in house	1	0
Bed	0	0
Birds	0	2
Blood	9	8
Bomb	0	0
Buildings (nonspecific)	1	0
Candles	0	0
Cannon	1	0
Casket	13	18
Clouds	2	2
Cross	2	11
Devil	1	1
Dirt	5	9
Dog	3	1
Electric outlet	0	0
Flowers/wreath	3/2	12/5
Fork	0	0
Funeral home	4	2
Gallows	2	0
Glasses	0	0
Grass	5	12
Gun	0	0
Hats	0	0
Hearse	0	0

Response Type	Males (n = 46)	Females (n = 61)
Hearts and tears	5	19
Horse	0	0
House	0	0
Hospital	0	0
Insect (e.g., bee)	0	0
Knife	6	4
Mask	3	0
Monster	5	1
Moon	1	0
Mountain	0	0
Orange sucker	0	0
Parachute	0	0
Plane	0	0
Policeman	0	0
Rain	0	0
Rope	2	0
Shovel	0	0
Sky	3	5
Snake	0	0
Snow	0	0
Squirrel	0	0
Stars	0	0
Sun	4	5
TV	0	0
Tank	0	0
Thunder	0	0
Tombstone	9	13
Trees	2	7
Vehicles (cars, ambulances)	1	1
Water	1	3
Windows/doors	1	0
Actions associated with death		
Attacked by a monster	0	0
Attacked by snakes	0	0
Being buried: in the ground	0	0
in a box	0	0
Being scared	2	0
Being separated	0	0
Being sick (e.g., heart attack)	12	13
Bleeding	0	0
Blood sucking (e.g., by a vampire)	0	0
Bombing/war	1	0
Car accident	1	1
Crucifixion	2	1

Response Type	Males (n = 46)	Females (n = 61)
Drowning	0	2
Electrocution	3	0
Falling	1	2
Fire	1	1
Guillotine	2	0
Hanging	2	0
Hitting	1	0
Hurting	0	0
Kidnapping	0	0
Old Age	8	10
Rack	1	0
Shooting	2	1
Smoking	0	0
Stabbing	7	5
Suicide	0	1
Not described	26	42

The reader should note that more than one method associated with the death of figure(s) in the children's drawings may be found in each drawing.

Who Killed Whom?

	Sex of Person/Animal Killed				
Sex of Killer	M	F	?	Death	Animal
M	3	1	0	0	1
F	0	0	0	0	0
?	24	5	8	1	1
Death	0	0	5	0	0
Not mentioned = 51					

5

Concluding Thoughts

The Child's Changing Conceptions

The dynamic pattern of the child's conceptions about death finds its origins in a magical-cyclical perspective that emphasizes the interchangeability of life and death. Children from 3 through 5 years of age understand death as a living on under changed circumstances. Death for these children also can be a separation from others; in particular, the mother. The next apparent stage in the process of acquiring conceptions about death is one in which death is personified. Death for children 6 through 8 years of age is seen as an external agent who can catch you and take you away. If you are young and healthy, and can see death coming at you in time, you can escape. This external agent can be ghostlike, monstrous, and even invisible. Personifications of death are found in conjunction with a growing interest in the rites of burial. The child is thought to conclude his journey toward adultlike standards when he sees death as the end of life, as scary or painful, or in abstract terms, such as a great blackness. Children of 9 years of

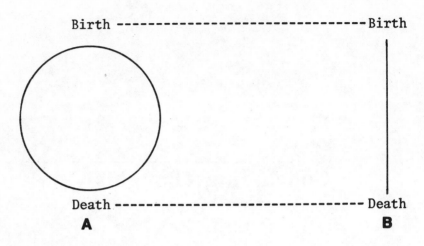

Figure 5–1. A schematic showing the cyclical and linear views of birth and death.

age and older can be described as having reached this level of conceptualization. They also are concerned with the rites of burial and with what happens to the body after death. Each of these three stages emerges out of the one preceding it, incorporating the earlier stage.

Figure 5–1 attempts to explain what seems to have happened over time to the conceptions of death held by children. Let us assume that a circle (A) represents the young child's view of birth and death, while a straight line (B) represents the views held by older children and adults.

The circle contains the unity of what might be seen by adults as apparent opposites, which are continually moving, changing one into the other and back again. It is a conceptual system, devoid of causality. There are no discrete beginning and end points, and no finality. There is only the flowing of birth into death and death into birth. The young child is part of this unity of apparent opposites, for he can neither separate himself from the world nor pull apart and segregate the subjective-objective components of the world.

With the passage of years, the circle is projected 90° so that to the eye of the older child and adult the circle now appears as a straight line that is bounded by birth at one end and death at the other. The viewer of this line has gone through a rigorous socialization and educational processing. Because of the strong role that causal models play in such processing, he now cannot see that it is really a circle viewed from an improper position. The rhythmic changes of the circle are replaced by the discreteness of the beginning and end of life. Causal explanations play an important role in teaching the child the nature of the relationships of all points on this "line of life," especially between the beginning and end points. What happens before birth and after death are the great unknowns, for the straight line tells us little about what happens "before or after."

The position can be taken that children and adults do not really differ in their conceptions about death; it is simply that younger children are more tolerant of seeming ambiguities. This offers another explanation of the observed changes in children's conceptions about death. To an extent, this argument suggests that a circular perspective is associated with greater tolerance for ambiguity than is a linear-causal perspective. To be adultlike in one's thinking, therefore, is to demonstrate concern about the regularities of existence and about lawful relationships, and to avoid the irregularities.

There is a regrettable lack of literature dealing with children's conceptions of aging. There exists as well a lack of agreement about the age or maturational level at which the child achieves an understanding of what has come to be called "futurity." It is estimated that the child attains time-related concepts during the period from late childhood through early adolescence. This new awareness is of the future being somehow different from the present. The knowledge of how the present differs from the past is joined by learning to hope for things to come and being concerned about the passage of time. Time becomes something to be used, to be put between one's life and the death awaiting in old age.

The 9-to-12 year old is said to be in the last phases of a process of giving up animistic-magical thinking in favor of logical-causal modes of analyzing the events of the world. This shift in thinking is accompanied by the child's gains in understanding the nature of external time. Knowledge of measured time becomes a signpost of the child's interest in using logical rather than magical models in his attempts to deal with his experiences and perceptions of the world.

It has been written that adolescents tend to be future-oriented to such an extent that they feel that they are constantly in a state of hurrying to get "somewhere." The near future holds this "somewhere," as they are said to give almost no thought to what might happen to them when they reach the age of 40 and move on into their geriatric years (Kastenbaum, 1959).

Similar findings were obtained when college students (mean age of 24.6 years) in my class on the Psychology of Aging, Dying and Death were asked to complete a lifeline exercise. In this exercise, students were asked to draw a line to represent their total lifespan and mark off on it the ages at which important events had occurred and might occur, and to describe those events. The years beyond 40 were almost devoid of any activities or events but retirement, loneliness, illness, and death, while the years before 40 were full and exciting.

It has been thought that those who are future-oriented as adolescents express fears of death, for death would cut them off from their future, and so they place as much time as possible between themselves and death. Preadolescents indicate that they expect to die between about 70 and 100 years, but we are uncertain if they also feel that their lives will be barren beyond 40 years of age. Perhaps the age of 40 years represents the time of social death, while the years beyond are reserved for physical death.

Borkeneau (1955) has put forth the proposition that attitude changes for individuals in a society serve as monitors of progress toward, or regression away from, prevailing social norms. When the child reaches the conclusion that death and aging are inevitable and universal, he has moved closer toward adult status, but the question of whether this achievement is to be valued or not has been passed over. Borkeneau further asserts that a culture's uncertainties about the relationships between life and death are reflected in their burial rites and interests in burial. We have seen such uncertainties through the changes in children. The 3-to-5 year old sees death as life under changed circumstances, and hence burial is only a temporary state of affairs. The 6-to-8 year old shows concern about proper burial rituals. The 9-to-12 year old sees death in biological and, at times, abstract terms. For this latter group of children, burial is now a permanent state of affairs.

The children we have discussed, and the cultures studied by Borkeneau seem to have ended with a view of death that is in opposition to the one they started out with. This new perspective for the older child carries with it feelings about the mortality of the self. In their early childhood, children believe only the old can die, not children. They come to learn that children do die, as do their parents.

The Child's Experiences with Death

The Fatally Ill Child

This story was dictated to her mother by a girl 8 years, 11 months old. One week later, she died.

> *Chapter 1.* One sunny day in 1964, a new dime was born. He was nice and round and shiny and so he was called Silver. Silver was put into a large sack where he met lots of relatives. He also made a friend. His friend was a penny. His name was Copper. Copper told Silver that he had been sitting in the sack for almost a year because there were lots of sacks ahead of theirs that would go to the bank ahead of them. Copper and Silver played in the sack for a few days, then "ding, ding," the door of the safe opened and in walked the bank manager, Mr. Wilson. He had come to get some money to take to the bank. Lo and behold, their sack was picked up with a jerk! All the coins jingled and jangled in the bag.

Copper and Silver wondered what was going to happen to them. All the way to the bank in the car they talked about what they thought it would be like in the big world. They were frightened but excited too.

Chapter 2. When they reached the bank, the car stopped with a jerk. Mr. Wilson got out and took the sacks of money into the bank. In the bank, Copper and Silver were separated because all the coins were put into separate drawers. Copper was in a drawer with lots of other pennies. Silver was in a drawer with lots of other dimes. Copper was very sad. He missed his friend Silver. Silver wished that he was with Copper. He didn't think that the bank was a very nice place to be if it was going to separate friends. Just then the bank door opened and in rushed Mrs. Smith. She was in a big hurry because she did not want to miss the 3 o'clock plane to California. She needed some money to take with her to buy some good souvenirs to bring back to Vancouver. "Ding, ding," the cash drawers opened with Copper and Silver inside. Copper and Silver were scooped out with a swish and put into Mrs. Smith's change-purse. They were together again!

Chapter 3. The sun was very hot in California. Copper and Silver almost melted. Then they heard Mrs. Smith calling "Taxi! Taxi!" and a car came rolling down the street. Mrs. Smith got in and told the driver to take her to the Pillers Inn. It was a bumpity ride and Copper and Silver jingled and jangled in Mrs. Smith's change-purse. They spent many happy days in Mrs. Smith's purse until the very last day, when she was leaving. She reached into her purse and pulled out both Copper and Silver to pay her bill. Just then in came John, the innkeeper's son. He asked for 11¢ to buy a chocolate bar. His Dad gave him Copper and Silver. John put them in his pocket, with a piece of string, a chunk of bubblegum and a dead snake. What a *mess!*

Chapter 4. Copper and Silver didn't like lying next to a snake. They looked around. There was a small hole. They gently slipped down the hole, rolled down his leg and came out the bottom of his pants, landing in the middle of the sidewalk. Silver said to Copper, "It sure is good to get away from that snake." Just then a little girl came walking down the sidewalk and saw them lying there in the sunshine. The little girl was Susan. She picked them up and put them in her pocket. There were much nicer things in her pocket than in Johnny's. There was a handkerchief with a flower on it, a comb and a piece of chocolate-covered candy. She rushed home and called out "Mommy, Mommy, guess what I found?" Her mother said, "What did you find?" "I found a dime and a penny from Canada," said Susan. She ran to her room and put them in her piggy bank, where she was saving her money for a trip to Shuswap Lake in Canada.

Chapter 5. Later that summer, Susan and her family took a long drive to Shuswap Lake. Copper and Silver were in her purse that smelled of perfume. They were happy to be going home to Canada. At the lake, Susan went to a small store to buy some penny suckers. She gave Copper to the storekeeper. Poor Silver, he lay in her purse all alone. His friend was gone again. As she walked out of the store, in came Billy. He wanted a bottle of pop. He gave the storekeeper 15¢ and got three pennies back. Copper was one of them. Now Copper was sure that he would never see Silver again. He didn't know that Silver was having an adventure of his own. Silver and Susan had gone down to the wharf to watch the men who were fishing. Susan bent over—her purse fell out of her hand—Silver rolled out of the purse and *splash!* into the water. A big fish came swimming by. He just loved shiny things. Here was the shiniest thing he had ever seen. With a big gulp he swallowed Silver up. Silver was sure he would never see Copper again. It was bony and dirty and sticky and smelly inside of the fish. He was very unhappy.

Chapter 6. The next day, Billy went fishing with his father. Billy was a good fisherman. He used a shiny bait. The old fish who had swallowed Silver came along and saw the shiny bait floating in the water. He opened his big mouth and grabbed the bait. Billy felt a *big* tug on his rod. He pulled it up and saw his reward—a great big fish, the biggest he had ever caught. His father sat there with his mouth opened and his eyes big. "Billy," he said, "What a good supper we will have tonight!" So they went home with a big grin on each of their faces. As Billy's Dad was cleaning out the fish, Billy saw something shiny. He ran and got a pair of tweezers so his father could get the shiny thing out of the fish. "It's a dime," yelled Billy. "That really was a good catch, I will put this dime in my coin collection," Billy said. "I also have three pennies; I will put one of them in my collection too." He picked one of the pennies out of his pocket. It was Copper! Into the coin book went Copper, and who was there beside him but his friend Silver. They would never be separated again. Billy had brought the friends together once again. THE END.

Research into the mental life of the terminally ill child is virtually nonexistent. Hoffman and Futterman (1971) remarked on this lack by pointing out that we have very little to go on when faced with the "abysmal aura" that surrounds the prognosis of a fatal illness. This is, no doubt, a function of the intense emotion and trauma associated with a child's fatal diagnosis (for the patient, the patient's family, and, to a lesser extent, the researcher). Reluctance to approach this topic also may have resulted from the belief that the fatally ill child does not have the intellectual ability to grasp the significance of his diagnosis; or, if he actually could, such information would be so destructive as to warrant maintaining an atmosphere of what Margaret Mead might have called "isolated togetherness."

Early research by Natterson and Knudson (1960) and Morrissey (1963) provided insight into this sensitive area. Natterson and Knudson were concerned with the in-hospital behavior of 33 children who were terminally ill with cancer. On the basis of recorded observations made by hospital staff (physicians, nurses, school teacher, occupational therapist, and social worker), the authors isolated three sources of stress for the hospitalized dying child: (1) separation from the mother, (2) traumatic procedures, and (3) the deaths of other children.

Mother absence was the most frequent cause of distress for the hospitalized child under five years of age. The symptoms of this separation anxiety were irritability, withdrawal, regression, tantrums, and crying; they were most acute during the first days in hospital and tended to subside with the passage of time.

Painful medical procedures (vein punctures, and bone-marrow aspirations) also contributed to the child's distress, particularly in the 5-to-10 age group. Schowalter (1970) suggested that the child has difficulty understanding the cause of his disease and may interpret the pain of medical procedures as confirmation that he is being punished for real or imagined wrongdoings. The mother's presence did little to alleviate this "fear of mutilation" and its accompanying anxiety. In effect, death (and its implied separation from parents) may be preferable to the pain and discomfort of the seemingly endless array of tests. I recall an interview with a mother and her dying eight-year-old girl, in which the child calmly expressed her preference to "die and be with Jesus," rather than return to the hospital for chemotherapy.

Not surprisingly for those in the 6-to-12 age range, the death of another child was also cited as a source of stress. The disruptive influence of this experience is exacerbated by nervous hospital staff, who frequently offered minimal and inadequate explanations for the vacant bed. Older children may often identify with the deceased, particularly if they had similar diagnoses, and this provides a frightening foretaste of the limitations of one's own life. The depression and withdrawal, so characteristic of this "death anxiety," were not eased by the presence of the mother; furthermore, the execution of various medical procedures heightened this anxiety.

Morrissey's (1963) study of 50 children admitted to a pediatrics ward with a diagnosis of cancer or leukemia is methodologically similar to that of Natterson and Knudson. From medical charts, social service records, and research staff interview records, judgments were made with regard to the children's degree of anxiety, source of anxiety, awareness of diagnosis and prognosis, quantitative and qualitative parent participation, and overall hospital adjustment.

Results revealed that 50% of the children exhibited severe anxiety during the course of hospitalization, while 41% had slight, yet noticeable, anxiety. Consistent with Natterson and Knudson, separation anxiety was prominent in the younger children, while direct expressions of death anxiety were commonly attributed to the eldest. Morrissey did not discuss the fear of mutilation, as his sample of children aged six to ten was small. Generally, the children were unaware of both their diagnosis and prognosis; only 22% were classified as aware or suspicious of their diagnosis (78% were unaware, while 32% were aware or suspicious of their prognosis (68% were unaware). Finally, overall hospital adjustment was a function of the quality of parent participation in child care, not the quantity of such efforts. This latter finding is contradictory to the Natterson and Knudson data; they concluded that maternal involvement did not appreciably reduce fear of mutilation or death anxiety. It is unclear however, whether a distinction was made between the quantity and quality of the mother-child interaction.

The relationship between chronological age and the fears exhibited by the fatally ill child is strikingly similar to the previous account of the development of the concept of death in physically healthy children. Up until age five, the healthy child fears separation from his mother, as does his dying counterpart. Death for the six-to-nine year old is personified as capable of launching violent assaults on the child; the fear of hospital procedures or the fear of mutilation are the parallel fears of the terminally ill youngster. Finally, the older child, with his appreciation of the finality and universality of death, fears it.

Both the Natterson and Knudson study and the Morrissey study concluded that such concerns emerged as a function of the child's "maturation of consciousness"; he first develops an awareness of his mother, then of his own physical being, and then of himself as a separate entity in time. Understanding death was equated with one's ability to conceptualize its meaning and to verbally express this understanding. Recent authors are generally in agreement that older children facing impending death can be aware of their prognosis and express anxiety about their mortality. There is a consensus too, that the principal concerns of children under five years are separation, loneliness, and abandonment. The conclusion has been contested recently that fatally ill children of approximately six-to-ten years of age are not capable of intellectually appreciating the statement, "I will die," and thus face their impending death with equanimity and awareness.

Spinetta (1974) and Waechter (1971) have leveled criticism at Natterson and Knudson (1960) and Morrissey (1963) for their reliance on parent-staff observations of hospitalized children, as well as their lack of controls and their failure to distinguish the psychological impact of a fatal illness from that of chronic, nonfatal conditions and hospitalization. Spinetta (1974), for example, cites research indicating that hospitalized children generally show anxiety (as a function of age) related to separation, mutilation, and permanent loss of bodily function. In other words, such fears may not be unique to the terminally ill hospitalized child.

In an attempt to clarify this issue, Waechter (1971) studied 64 children (aged six to ten years) in four matched groups: 1) terminally ill, 2) nonfatal, chronically ill, 3) brief illnesses, and 4) normal, nonhospitalized. The first three groups were in hospital when tested. Since Waechter was interested in eliciting responses directly from the children, through fantasy and indirect expressions of the child's concerns with present and future body integration and functioning, each child was required to respond to a set of eight pictures. Four of the pictures were selected from the Thematic Apperception Test (Stein, 1955) and the remainder were designed specifically for this study. Interviews were also conducted with parents, to assess factors that might influence the quality and quantity of the child's concerns about death.

In contrast to the other group, those children with a terminal illness (n = 16) related more death themes (versus separation or mutilation) and told more stories involving threat to body integrity and functioning. More specifically, they frequently ascribed their diagnosis and symptoms to the character in the story. Waechter concluded that fatally ill children from six to ten years of age are more preoccupied with death than are their chronically ill peers, and they experience considerably more anxiety, although this may not be discernible unless one attends to subtle measures or indirect expressions of such concerns.

Spinetta, Rigler, and Karon (1973; cited by Spinetta, 1974) have added support to Waechter's conclusions. Twenty-five children hospitalized with leukemia and a similar number of children hospitalized with chronic but nonfatal illnesses (for example, diabetes or asthma) responded to (1) an anxiety questionnaire distinguishing home and hospital concerns and (2) a series of four pictures of hospital scenes. All respondents were in the six-to-ten age range.

Analyses revealed that terminally ill children had a heightened awareness of hospital experience, its personnel, and procedures. It is significant that the stories of the fatally ill related a preoccupation with threat to their bodies and interference with bodily functions. In contrast to the chronically ill children, those with leukemia also expressed more hospital-related and non hospital-related anxiety.

Bluebond-Langner (1974) proposed that terminally ill children pass through different stages of awareness about their illness. In the first of six stages, regardless of age, children realize the seriousness of their illness. This stage is followed by the child's observations of the side effects of the drugs he is taking, and his ability to name them. The child moves on to an understanding of the purpose of the treatment and procedures he is subjected to (Stage 3), and to an awareness of the cycles of relapses and remissions of his disease, still without incorporating his own possible death into these cycles (Stage 4). Death becomes a part of the child's disease cycle in Stage 5; in Stage 6, internalization of the fatal prognosis takes place. Bluebond-Langer suggests that going from Stages 2 through 5 takes some time, while going from Stage 5 to 6 could be achieved quickly if the child heard of the death of another child. She felt that each stage represented a greater understanding of the disease and its prognosis. This left the child with a great deal to cope with, and became part of his anticipatory grief process.

The evidence suggests, then, that relying solely on the terminally ill child's overt expressions of anxiety yields incomplete or misleading information. In fact, both Natterson and Knudson (1960) and Morrissey (1963) suggested the possibility that the younger child could express death concerns indirectly; however, their emphasis on parent-staff observations precluded consideration of such data. Spinetta (1974), after reviewing the literature, concluded that

> ". . . the fatally ill 6-to-10 year old child is concerned about his illness and that even though this concern may not always take the form of overt expressions about his impending death, the more subtle fears and anxieties are nonetheless real, painful, and very much related to the seriousness of the illness that the child is experiencing. Whether or not one wishes to call this anxiety of the

child about his own fatal illness, though not conceptualized, death anxiety, seems to be a problem of semantics rather than of fact." [p. 259]

In both the Waechter (1971) and Spinetta, Rigler, and Karon (1973) research, the leukemic children were *not* aware that their disease was fatal, yet from the first admission to hospital they had significantly higher levels of anxiety than matched, chronically ill children. Why? The answer lies in the nature of parent-child interactions. Even though the prognosis was not formally communicated to the child, the parents were informed of the inevitable course of the disease; the consequent disruption in family interactions caused by protracted dying revealed to the child that he had no "ordinary illness."

Care of the terminally ill child places enormous stress on each family member, often taxing one's resiliency to the limits. In a retrospective study of 20 leukemic families, Binger et al. (1969) found that (1) in 50% of the families, at least one member required psychiatric intervention; (2) the texture of family life was dramatically transformed, as divorce, academic, and behavioral problems frequently were reported; and (3) envy and jealousy often were expressed at the extensive parental attention to the dying member.

Natterson and Knudson (1960) reported that the mothers of fatally ill children responded initially with tenseness, anxiety, withdrawal, overt crying, denial, and the need for increased physical contact with their children. These reactions often lead to guilt-laden responses in which mothers wondered if they had done something wrong to precipitate their child's illness.

Sensitive management of the nonmedical needs of terminally ill children must consider both the intellectual capabilities of the child and the attitudes and feelings of those in his immediate environment. Anxious to protect the fatally ill child, parents all too frequently attempt to hide the nature and severity of the child's disease, believing that open discussion of the future would create tremendous, unmanageable anxiety and shatter already shaky, inadequate defenses. The child's expressions of his concerns are met with evasiveness; failing to find support and comfort, the child is left alone with his fantasies, which may be more destructive and frightening than the reality of his condition. This is a futile exercise, doomed to failure, and motivated principally out of the survivor's selfish concern. The parents, siblings, and certainly the terminally ill child, all need an atmosphere of support and encouragement, freeing them to express their fears and concerns. Such an environment is instrumental in alleviating death anxiety, as well as feelings of isolation and loneliness (Waechter, 1971; Bluebond-Langner, 1974).

Childhood Bereavement*

In addition to those children who suffer a fatal disease, other children also have contact with death and dying when someone they love dies. Early theorists attached much importance to the parent-child relationship (particularly the mother-child relationship; the traumatic rupture of this relationship was thought to leave an indelible and detrimental impact on the emerging personality of the young child. The reasons are not entirely clear, but many researchers did not study bereaved children; rather, they collected data from adults' retrospective reports of their own childhood bereavement and related this to adjustment in adult life. This section is an evaluation of the research into such issues as 1) whether or not parental death in childhood is associated with adult personality disturbance, 2) whether or not parental loss as a function of separation or divorce is more likely than parental loss through death to influence adult development, and 3) whether there is a critical age at which loss of a parent is particularly devastating to the child. The discussion will focus upon psychoneurosis, depression, and schizophrenia.

*This section was contributed by Steve Fleming and is gratefully acknowledged.

Psychoneurosis. The Barry and Lindemann (1960) study, emphasizing the "etiological" significance of maternal death in the development of neurotic behavior, stands in stark contrast to the bulk of research in this area. Consistent reports of parental divorce, separation, desertion, and psychiatric disturbance—not death—in the childhood experiences of neurotics indicate that childhood parental bereavement is not a major factor in the etiology of psychoneurotic disturbances (Brill and Liston, 1966; Munro and Griffiths, 1969; Pitts et al., 1965). Nor did these researchers confirm the Barry and Lindemann (1960) finding of a higher incidence of maternal death prior to age five (for female neurotics, prior to age two).

Depression. Brown (1961), in perhaps the most frequently cited study of the relationship between childhood parental bereavement and adult depression, compared the incidence of parental loss across 321 depressed outpatients and two control groups, statistics on orphanhood from the 1921 British Census and a sample of medical patients. Significantly more of the depressed suffered the death of one or both of their parents, and the loss of the father was particularly prominent.

Criticism has been leveled at Brown for using heterogeneous samples of depressed patients—that is, including under the rubric of "depression" such diverse diagnoses as involutional melancholia, agitated depresson, manic-depressive psychosis, and reactive depression. Indeed, when one examines the relationship between childhood bereavement and a homogeneous sample of depressed patients (in this instance, those diagnosed as manic-depressives), the data reveal no significant excess of parent loss in the clinical group, when compared with Brown's two control groups (Hopkinson and Reed, 1966).

While the data, although meager, do not suggest an association between childhood bereavement and adult depressive reactions, research examining the *severity* of depressed mood and childhood experiences has been more extensive and more productive. Beck, Sethi, and Tuthill (1963) classified 297 depressives as "high-depressed" or "low-depressed" on the basis of responses to a depression inventory and a clinical evaluation. Compared with nondepressed psychiatric controls and the low-depressed group, significantly more of those severely depressed reported the loss of a parent. Furthermore, loss of father is over-represented for high-depressed males and females.

Munro (1966) compared childhood bereavement experiences in patients suffering "primary depression" (those with " . . . no previous history of mental disorder other than affective illness or cyclothymic personality") with a matched control group of medical outpatients. The proportion of depressives who lost a parent by death was not significantly different from the controls. Although not statistically significant, depressives showed a tendency toward having experienced parental death between the ages of 11 and 15. There was no similar tendency for maternal loss.

Munro (1966) further differentiated the depressed patients on the basis of the severity of their disorder. Severe depression was diagnosed in the presence of one or more of the following factors: 1) presence of retardation, 2) delusions or guilt feelings, 3) no definite relationship to precipitating factors, and 4) recurrence or history of previous manic illness. When none of the above were present, the depression was considered to be moderate.

Considering the severity-of-depression variable, nearly twice as many severe and moderate depressives had lost a parent by death in childhood. Although not significant, the trend was for the severely depressed group to report a greater number of mothers lost in childhood. In a later study with inpatient and outpatient depressives (Munro and Griffiths, 1969), maternal loss was significantly higher in the inpatient group but not the outpatient sample.

There is evidence to suggest that childhood bereavement influences adult affective disturbance, but the precise nature of this association is unclear. The differential impact of a parent's death as a function of the sexes of the parent and child needs attention. The death of the father has been reported to adversely affect subsequent emotional adjustment of both sons and daughters

(Beck, Sethi, and Tuthill, 1963; Brown, 1961), particularly for the latter between the ages of 10 and 15. Maternal death also has been associated with adult depressive reaction (Munro, 1966), especially in daughters (Birtchnell, 1970). This confusion results from a number of factors, most notably the assortment of control groups used and the differing methods of distinguishing severely and moderately depressed patients.

Schizophrenia. The trend of early research results was to add support to the psychoanalytic notion that the death of a parent was an extremely traumatic event and a contributing factor in adult schizophrenic behavior (Barry, 1939; Barry and Bousfield, 1937; Berg and Cohen, 1959). As was the case in the discussion of childhood bereavement and neurotic disorders, subsequent research challenged the postulated crucial role of parental deprivation through death, and failed to support the existence of "critical periods" for parental death during one's early years (Granville-Grossman, 1966; Oltman, McGarry, and Friedman, 1952).

It is not the intent of this review to minimize the impact of the death of a child's parent; admittedly, this is a depressing and stressful time. What is being argued is that parental death is not of sole etiological import in the development of schizophrenia in adulthood. Rather, death is one form that parental deprivation might take; there are other equally distressing and destructive experiences. Separation from parents as a result of divorce or abandonment and a history of parental psychiatric disturbance both have been implicated in faulty adult adjustment. Oltman, McGarry, and Friedman (1952) compared the frequency of parental deprivation (by death, divorce, or psychosis) in a sample of schizophrenics and controls. For the controls, employees of the same psychiatric institution, death of the parent was the major source of deprivation; in the schizophrenic group, death actually was less prominent than deprivation by divorce and psychosis. For Brill and Liston (1966) the distinguishing characteristic of parental deprivation for the schizophrenic sample also was loss resulting from divorce or separation, not death.

In summary, there is evidence associating a variety of childhood stresses, notably divorce, separation, and parental psychiatric disturbance, with schizophrenic reactions in adulthood. In fact, this conclusion is given added credibility when one considers that the principal dissenting authors, such as Berg and Cohen (1959), have commented, albeit briefly, on these disruptive effects. There is also growing evidence that the relationship between the death of a parent in childhood and subsequent gross personality disturbance may be more complex than originally proposed.

A different research focus. The surge of research into the effects of childhood bereavement has been reduced to a trickle. What has been published lately continues to stress such variables as cause of loss, age at loss, and sexes of parent and child; however, research methodologies have changed substantially. One promising example of this line of research has been provided by Hetherington (1966, 1972), who actually observed children and adolescents from intact and disrupted homes in a variety of social interactions.

In her initial investigation, Hetherington (1966) examined the effects of father absence and time of departure of the father on the sex-typed behaviors of preadolescent males aged 9 to 12. Father separation was the result of divorce, desertion, death, or illegitimacy; no attempt was made to assess the differential impact of these various causes. These children, from intact and disrupted home environments, attended a recreation center. In addition to completing a test of sex-role preference, their recreation directors rated them on seven-point scales measuring dependence on adults, dependence on peers, independence, and aggression.

Both early-separated (before age five) and late-separated boys (after age five) were more dependent on peers than boys with fathers living at home. Although age at separation had no influence on the total independence and dependence on adult scales, it did affect sex-role preferences; boys separated from their fathers early were less aggressive, more "feminine" in their sex-role preferences, and participated less in physical games involving contact and more in nonphysical, noncompetitive activities. Participants separated from their fathers after age five and those from intact homes were similar in their levels of aggressive behavior and in their sex-role preferences.

These results led Hetherington to hypothesize that adequate masculine identification had occurred by age six, and that this identification could be maintained in the absence of the father. Furthermore, if paternal absence occurred in the first four years (before identification could be adequately established), long-lasting disruption in sex-typed behaviors might result.

In a more comprehensive investigation of the impact of father absence, Hetherington (1972) turned her attention to adolescent girls (13 to 17 years). Reason for paternal separation also was explored, as the distinction was made between father absence due to divorce or death. In contrast to the previous research with preadolescent boys, father absence did not affect sex-typed behavior or preferences, nor did it influence the girls' relations with other females. Nonverbal measures recorded during interviews revealed that loss of father had an impact on female adolescents' behaviors with males; the cause of father absence was an important consideration.

With a male interviewer, daughters who had lost their fathers through death spoke infrequently, avoided proximity with the interviewer in seat selection and body orientation, and maintained rigid postural characteristics. The behavior of daughters who had lost their fathers through divorce was in marked contrast. They were open and receptive with the interviewer, seeking proximity, and smiling. Daughters of divorcees also reported earlier dating and sexual intercourse; daughters of widows started dating later and were sexually inhibited. Finally, the earlier the paternal separation occurred, the greater the disparity between these two groups.

Hetherington offers evidence to suggest that father separation has a different impact on sons than on daughters, and that age at the time of loss is an influential variable. Further, paternal loss due to divorce or separation may well have more potential for maladjustment than the death of one's father.

We have not discussed in detail *why* childhood bereavement

should be associated with adult personality disturbance in the first place, and with good reason. One of the salient characteristics of this area of investigation is the virtual absence of any comprehensive theoretical base or model from which to launch one's research efforts. It was the tendency of psychoanalytical theorists to equate mourning for a loved object with depression, and this led to the association of childhood bereavement with depression. Even so, it is not precisely clear why one also would expect such an experience to influence the emergence of adult schizophrenic or psychoneurotic disorders. It is lamentable, too, that those who suggested hypotheses for a childhood bereavement-personaltiy disorder association, whether it be psychoanalytic, heredo-constitutional, or functional, exhibited such an obsession with one research paradigm. With slight modification, the tradition was to compare frequencies of parental separation or death in psychiatric and nonpsychiatric samples.

Separation from one's parent(s), whether by death, divorce, or separation, is an exceedingly difficult time for the child; however, such experiences do not invariably lead to severe personality disturbances in adulthood. Unfortunately, much of the past research has stressed the disruptive impact of parental deprivation. A more productive research emphasis would have less reliance on psychiatric patients and concentrate on identifying those factors, in the present and past environments of the bereaved or separated child, that enhance adjustment and those that detract from it. Hilgard, Newman, and Fisk (1960), for example, have reported that keeping the home intact and the use of support systems (relatives, the community, and church resources) by the mother assisted in the childhood adjustment of women whose fathers had died. The mother's continued and excessive dependency on her children and premature remarriage were factors that hindered adjustment.

The over-reliance on retrospective methods of data collection has failed to unlock the complexity of the child's response to parental separation. Hetherington (1966, 1972) has clearly demonstrated the need for controlled laboratory and participant observation procedures; she also has illustrated, through her use of multiple-response measures, the subtle nature of the interpersonal and intrapersonal effects of parental death or separation. Hetherington also tested bereaved children and adolescents, something other researchers have been reluctant to do.

With few exceptions (Brown, 1961; Hilgard, Newman, and Fisk, 1960), authors have consistently ignored, in the interpretation of their results, the previously discussed data on children's attitudes towards death. The child's attitudes toward death, and his responses to a parent's death, do not develop in a vacuum but must be considered against the backdrop of his/her emotional, cognitive, and social experience.

Chetnik (1970) presented the case of a six-year-old boy, Mark, whose mother was dying, and did die, of cancer. The boy had been in therapy for seven months prior to the announcement of his mother's condition. This treatment was brought about by his aggressiveness and negative emotional reactions toward his mother. At the onset of her illness and throughout her periods of hospitalization, Mark was assessed as not being able to appraise the situation; he denied and fantasized it instead. As his mother recovered, he was able to "see" her as a mother figure again and became able to express more positive feelings toward her.

He gave his mother a "heart book" as an expression of his revised feelings. The book began with "Mommie, Mommie, I don't want you to be sick. I don't want to get angry with you and have a fight" (p. 630). In his book he then went on to ask such questions about death as; "What makes people die?" and "Do they have boxes (caskets) for children?"

Care should be taken in extending this case, but we also should be prepared to accept the information contained in personal accounts with some reasonable and, it is hoped, relevant framework, no matter how personal.

Mark reacted to the dying of his mother with a combination of anger and helplessness. His anger and fear were over the changes in her brought on by the illness, changes that made her less and less like "his mother." If she could be changed, lose her identity, could it also happen to him? Mark's mother ceased to be "his mother" when she was ill. Death is to be raged against, for it is a loss of self, a change into another being, and can bring about both feelings of driving aggressiveness and paralyzing helplessness (McConville et al., 1970; Mitchell, 1967).

Chetnik compares the case of Mark with the findings of Rochlin (1953) and Shambaugh (1961) and concludes that where the child's dependency needs on a parent are so strong that he must deny the loss of a parent, then mourning could not be expected to take place. The strength of the dependency of the child on a parent may be interpreted as being a warm and loving relationship, but it also can interfere with the processes of mourning and their influences on the child and the other members of the family.

When the death of a family member occurs, the child may not use fantasy; instead, aspects of the death are selectively forgotten or avoided. An actual death experience for the child also can stimulate the development of more mature concepts about death that do not follow a proscribed pattern (Anthony, 1973). As an example, Anthony presents the case of Irene M. (7 years, 8 months) whose father died. Through analysis of Irene's definitions of "dead" and responses to the story completion test, it was discovered that she could produce no fantasies about her dead father, but could fantasize about her mother's death, even though her mother was still alive. She could identify with her mother, as could have been predicted from the work of Markusen and Fulton (1971). In fact, Anthony goes on to demonstrate that Irene held her father in some degree of contempt. This was unaltered by his death, nor did she show a sense of guilt or fear of punishment over his death. As a final note in this case, Irene showed a fear of her own shadow, which was interpreted to mean that she feared her own death, for the shadow was an externally projected death anxiety. Fear of one's own shadow has a long history; documentation by the Greeks shows that they referred to the dead as "the shadows."

The literature on the reactions of children to the death of a parent or sibling has shown that children can manifest disturbances in both their affective and cognitive functioning (Barnes, 1964; Cain, Cain and Fast, 1966; Cain, Cain, and Erickson, 1964; Furman, 1964a,b; Rosenblatt, 1967). This work also has tended to point out the need for more effective therapeutic interventions for the bereaved and disturbed child. The view as expressed by Rosenblatt (1967) suggested that the only way to prevent the emotionally debilitating consequences of the death of a family member was to do away with death itself.

Talking about Death

Parents tend to experience a good deal of frustration and helplessness when faced with questions about death from their children, whether healthy or fatally ill (Karon and Vernick, 1968; Hoffman and Futterman, 1971; Kavanaugh, 1972). The avoidance of discussions about death seems to arise out of the need of many parents to impress their children with their confidence and knowledge of life. They feel that it is unwise to appear confused, uncertain, or frightened in front of their children. Discussions about death are necessary, however, and should recognize and respect the unique reactions and choices of children while helping them to develop concepts of personal existence.

Despite some spirited efforts directed at not talking with children about death, their fantasies and games demonstrate that they have learned more than we may care to give them credit for. The pressures for "not telling" about death suggest that such discussions challenge and oppose the strong associations we have built between children and life. Such a shortsighted approach forgets the historical associations children have had with death (Bakan, 1966). A tighter and tighter web of institutionalized protections has been created to keep the realities of existence not only from children but from adults as well. For example, Kastenbaum (1977) has reported that 70% of college students had not seen a dead person up close, 92% had not witnessed a death; while Fulton (1973) has noted that approximately 65% of reported deaths occur in the hospital.

Our not informing children about death has become part of an avoidance of coping with crises. This avoidance is bound strongly to the feeling that life can neutralize death. Freud suggested that this neutralization is only temporary, and that the "death instinct" will break out again to conquer life. The important issue here is not whether Freudian interpretations are correct or not, but whether or not questions about existence arise and, if so, are discussed.

> I sometimes get an urge to shoot or at least soundly spank all who taught me fear was evil or somehow less than human. . . . I found that those around me who were not busy running from their fears could be my closest and most effective friends as death came near.
>
> Kavanaugh, 1972, p. 57

It might be easier to talk with children about death if enough people came back from the dead to tell us what it was like, and some recent literature has provided such accounts (Moody, 1976; Currie, 1978). If we knew more about the effects of death education on children's conceptual development, it also might ease our anxiety about discussing death. Kavanaugh (1972) noted that if we neglect the death education of children, we allow them the "time and opportunity to sift their own data, to learn puzzling and fearful interpretations elsewhere, while concocting weird fantasies that may affect their lifelong attitudes toward mortality" (p. 128).

Discussions of death with children should include considerations of life as well, and be guided by the child's curiosity. The family has, for the most part, borne the responsibility for these discussions. Parents must be able to deal with their own fears of death in order to create an atmosphere for telling and coping; this is of particular importance in the case of fatally ill children (Hoffman and Futterman, 1971). Parents also must learn to balance their own fears against their knowledge of the family as a source of love for their child, in order to insure that they do not get locked into a state of passive noncommunication with their children over issues of concern to all of them. Exchange of information between parent and child can be threatening to the child, as it can arouse anxiety about future events and can make parents quite uncomfortable. Information also can be comforting when the realities it portrays are less fearful than fantasies. The goal of discussions with children becomes one of helping them, and ourselves, to live more freely.

Discussions must be honest and not merely aid in the creation of alternative myths. (Perhaps there is no better story about how facing death honestly beautifies life than is found in Rilke's *Stories About the Good God*.) Discussion must allow the child to make appropriate deductions and to help parents to come to some better understanding of their child's concepts. Some factors to consider in discussions with children are:

1. Did the child have any experience with the aged and/or with death?
2. Is the child aware of the imminent death of a person he knows?
3. Is the child fatally ill?

Guidelines for "telling" have been provided by Jackson (1965), Galen (1972), Kavanaugh (1972), Vernick and Lunceford (1967), Hoffman and Futterman (1971), Best (1948), Berg and Daugherty (1972), Wolf (1973), Le Shan (1976), Grollman (1967), and Fassler (1978), and can be summarized as follows:

1. Children are ready and capable of talking about anything within their own experience.
2. Use the language of the child, not the sentimental symbols we find so easy to utter.
3. Don't expect an immediate and obvious response from the child.
4. Be a good listener and observer.
5. Don't try to do it all in one discussion; that is, be available.
6. Make certain that your child knows that he is part of the family, especially when a death has occurred.
7. One of the most valuable methods of teaching children about death is to allow them to talk freely and ask their own questions.

To bring this chapter to a close, Budmen's (1969) brief but compelling statement about the death education of children is most appropriate:

> . . . most of a child's education is for life which leaves him help-less in dealing with death. Such neglect is inexcusable and unnec-essary. [pp. 11–12]

References

Alexander, I.E. and Adlerstein, A.M. 1958. Affective responses to the concept of death in a population of children and early adolescents. *Journal of Genetic Psychology, 3:* 167–177.

Almy, M.; Chittenden, E.; and Miller, P. 1966. *Young children's thinking: Studies of some aspects of Piaget's thinking.* New York: Teacher's College Press.

Alschuler, R.H. and Hattwick, B.W. 1947. *Painting and personality: A study of young children.* Chicago: University of Chicago Press.

Amstutz, J. 1973. Personal communication.

Amstutz, J. 1978. Personal communication.

Anthony, S. 1940. *The child's discovery of death.* New York: Harcourt, Brace, Jovanovich.

Anthony, S. 1973. *The discovery of death in childhood and after.* London: Penguin. (Revision of *The child's discovery of death.* New York: Harcourt, Brace, Jovanovich, 1940).

Argyris, C. 1968. Some unintended consequences of rigorous research. *Psychological Bulletin, 70:* 185–197.

Aries, P. 1962. *Centuries of childhood*. New York: Alfred A. Knopf.

Bakan, D. 1966. *The duality of human existence*. Chicago: Rand McNally and Co.

Barnes, M.J. 1964. *Reaction to the death of mother: The psychoanalytic study of the child*, pp. 334–358. New York: International Universities Press.

Baring-Gould, W.S. and Baring-Gould, C. 1962. *The annotated mother goose*. New York: Bramwell House.

Barry, H., Jr. and Bousfield, W.A. 1937. Incidence of orphanhood among 1500 psychiatric patients. *Journal of Genetic Psychology, 50:* 198–201.

Barry, H., Jr. 1939. A study of bereavement: An approach to problems in mental disease. *American Journal of Orthopsychiatry, 9:* 355–360.

Barry, H., Jr. and Lindemann, E. 1960. Critical ages for maternal bereavement in psychoneurosis. *Psychosomatic Medicine, 22:* 166–181.

Beck. A.T.; Sethi, B.; and Tuthill, R.W. 1963. Childhood bereavement and adult depression. *Archives of General Psychiatry, 9:* 295–302.

Becker, H. and Bruner, D.K. 1931. Attitude toward death and the dead and some possible causes of ghost fear. *Mental Hygiene, 15*(4): 828–837.

Berg, C.D. and Daugherty, G. 1972. Teaching about death. *Journal of the National Education Association, 62:* 46–47.

Berg, M. and Cohen, B. 1959. Early separation from the mother. *Journal of Nervous and Mental Disorders, 128:* 365–369.

Berman, S. and Laffal, J. 1953. Body type and figure drawing. *Journal of Clinical Psychology, 9:* 368–370.

Best, P. 1948. An experience in interpreting death to children. *Journal of Pastoral Care, 2:* 29–34.

Binger, C.M.; Ablin, A.R.; Feurstein, R.C.; Kushner, J.H.; Zoger, S.; and Mikkelsen, C. 1969. Childhood leukemia: Emotional impact on patient and family. *New England Journal of Medicine, 280:* 414–418.

Birtchnell, J. 1970. Early parent death and mental illness. *British Journal of Psychiatry, 116:* 281–288.

Bluebond-Langner, M. 1974. I know, do you? A study of awareness, communication, and coping in terminally ill children. In *Anticipating grief,* eds. B. Schoenberg; A.C. Carr; A.H. Kutscher; D. Peretz; and I. Goldberg; pp. 171–181. New York: Columbia University Press.

Blum, G.S and Rosensweig, S. 1944. The incidence of sibling and parental deaths in the anamnesis of female schizophrenics. *Journal of Genetic Psychology, 31:* 3–13.

Borkeneau, F. 1955. The concept of death. *The 20th Century, 157:* 313–329.

Bowlby, J. 1969. *Attachment.* New York: Basic Books.

Bowlby, J. 1973. *Separation.* New York: Basic Books.

Brill, N. and Liston, E. 1966. Parental loss in adults with emotional disorders. *Archives of General Psychiatry, 14:* 307–314.

Britton, E.C. and Winaus, J.M. 1958. *Growing from infancy to adulthood.* New York: Appleton-Century-Crofts.

Brown, D.G. and Tolor, A. 1957. Human figure drawings as indicators of sexual identification and inversion. *Perceptual and Motor Skills, 7:* 199–211.

Brown, E.A. and Goitein, P.L. 1943. The significance of body image for personality assay. *Journal of Nervous and Mental Disorders, 97:* 401–408.

Brown, F. 1961. Depression and childhood bereavement. *British Journal of Psychiatry, 107:* 754–777.

Brown, F. 1966. Childhood bereavement and subsequent psychiatric disorder. *British Journal of Psychiatry, 112:* 1035–1041.

Buck, J.N. 1948. The H-T-P test. *Journal of Clinical Psychology, 4:* 151–159.

Budmen, K.O. 1969. Grief and the young: A need to know. *Archives of the Foundation of Thanatology*, 1: 11–12.

Buhler, K. 1930. *The mental development of the child*. London: Routledge and Kegan Paul.

Buhler, C.; Smitter, F.; and Richardson, S. 1952. *Childhood problems and the teacher*. New York: Holt, Rinehart and Winston.

Cain, A.C.; Cain, B.S.; and Erickson, M.E. 1964. Children's disturbed reactions to the death of a sibling. *American Journal of Orthopsychiatry*, 34: 741–752.

Cain, A.C.; Cain, B.S.; and Fast, I. 1966. Children's disturbed reactions to parent suicide. *American Journal of Orthopsychiatry*, 36: 873–880.

Caprio, F.S. 1950. A study of some psychological reactions during prepubescence to the idea of death. *Psychiatric Quarterly*, 24: 495–505.

Cassirer, E. 1953. *An essay on Man*. New York: Doubleday.

Castaneda, C. 1972. *Journey to Ixtlan*. New York: Simon and Schuster.

Chadwick, M. 1929. Notes upon the fear of death. *International Journal of Psychoanalysis*, 10: 321–334.

Chaffee, S.H. and McLeod, J.M. 1972. Adolescent television use in the family context. In *Television and social behaviors, Vol. 3.*, eds. G.A. Comstack, E.A. Rubenstein and J.P. Murray. Washington, D.C.: U.S. Government Printing Office.

Chetnik, M. 1970. The impact of object loss on a six-year-old. *Journal of the American Academy of Child Psychiatry*, 9(4): 624–643.

Chien, I. September 3, 1967. Verity vs. truth in the scientific enterprise. Invited address to the Division of Philosophical Psychology at the Annual Meeting of the American Psychological Association.

Childers, P. and Wimmer, M. 1971. The concept of death in early childhood. *Child Development*, 42: 705–712.

Cohen, J.; Hansel, C.E.M.; and Sylvester, J. 1954. An experimental study of comparative judgments of time. *British Journal of Psychology, 45:* 108–114.

Currie, I. 1978. *You cannot die.* Toronto: Metheun Publications.

Debuskey, M. 1970. Orchestration of care. In *The chronically ill child and his family,* ed. M. Debuskey. Springfield, Ill.: Charles C Thomas.

De Dellarossa, G.S. 1965. The concept of death in your self-development. *Revista de Psicoanalisis, 22:* 26–44.

Easson, W.M. 1970. *The dying child: The management of the child or adolescent who is dying.* Springfield, Ill.: Charles C Thomas.

England, A.O. 1943. The psychological study of children's drawings. *American Journal of Orthopsychiatry, 13:* 525–531.

Erikson, E. 1950. *Childhood and society.* New York: Norton.

Eron, L.D.; Lefkowitz, M.M.; Huessmann, L.R.; and Walder, L.Q. 1972. Does television violence cause aggression? *American Psychologist, 27:* 253–263.

Fassler, J. 1978. *Helping children cope.* New York: The Free Press.

Feshback. S. and Singer, R.D. 1971. *Television and aggression: An experimental field study.* San Francisco: Josey-Bass.

Fiefel, H. 1959. *The meaning of death.* New York: McGraw-Hill.

Fiefel, H. 1976. Religious conviction and fear of death among the healthy and terminally ill. In *Death and identity,* ed. R. Fulton, pp. 120–130. Maryland: Charles Press Publishers.

Fontana, V.J. 1964. *The maltreated child.* Springfield, Ill.: Charles C Thomas.

French, J.E. 1952. Children's preferences for pictures of varied complexity of pictorial pattern. *Elementary School Journal, 53:* 90–95.

Freud, A. and Burlingham, D.T. 1943. *War and children.* New York: Medical War Books.

Freud, S. 1955. Total and taboo (1912–13). In *The Complete Psychological Works of Sigmund Freud*, ed. J. Strachey. London: Hogarth Press.

Freud, S. 1957. *Thoughts for the times on war and death*. London: Hogarth Press and the Institute for Psychoanalysis.

Fulton, R. 1973. Death and dying: Some sociological aspects of terminal care. *Modern Medicine of Canada, 28:* 112–115.

Furman, R.A. 1964 (a). Death of a six-year-old's mother during his analysis. *The Psychoanalytic Study of the Child, 19:* 379–393.

Furman, R.A. 1964 (b). Death and the young child: Some preliminary considerations. *Psychoanalytic Study of the Child, 19:* 321–333.

Futterman, E.H. and Hoffman, I. 1970. Shielding from awareness: An aspect of family adaptation to fatal illness in children. *Archives of Thanatology, 2:* 23–24.

Galen, H. 1972. A matter of life and death. *Young Children, 27:* 351–356.

Gardner, D.B. 1969. *Development in early childhood*. New York: Harper and Row.

Gasgrek, K.A. 1951. A study of the consistency and the reliability of certain of the formal and structural characteristics of children's drawings. Unpublished doctoral dissertation, Columbia University.

Gerbner, G. 1972. Violence in television dramas: Trends and symbolic functions. In *Television and social behavior, Vol.1.* eds. G.A. Comstock, E.A Rubenstein, and J.P. Murray. Washington, D.C.: U.S. Government Printing Office.

Gesell, A. 1954. The ontogenesis of infant behavior. In *Manual of Child Psychology, Ed. 2,* ed. L. Carmichael. New York: John Wiley and Sons.

Gesell, A. et al. 1940. *The first five years of life*. New York: Harper and Row.

Gesell, A. and Ilg, F.L. 1943. *Infant and child in culture today*. New York: Harper and Row.

Gesell, A. and Ilg, F.L. 1946. *The child from five to ten*. New York: Harper and Row.

Gesell, A. and Ilg, F.L. 1949. *Child development: An introduction to the study of human development*. New York: Harper and Row.

Gesell, A.: Ilg, F.L.; and Ames, L.B. 1956. *Youth: the years ten to sixteen*. New York: Harper and Row.

Gibson, J.L. 1966. *The senses considered as perceptual systems*. Boston, Mass.: Houghton-Mifflin Co.

Glueck, S. and Glueck, E. 1950. *500 delinquent boys: Unravelling juvenile delinquency*. New York: Commonwealth Fund.

Goodenough, F.L. 1926. *Measurement of intelligence by drawings*. New York: Harcourt, Brace, Jovanovich.

Granville-Grossman, R. 1966. Early bereavement and schizophrenia. *British Journal of Psychiatry, 112*: 1027–1034.

Greenberger, E. 1965. Fantasies of women confronting death. *Journal of Consulting Psychology, 29*: 252–260.

Grollman, E.A., ed. 1967. *Explaining death to children*. Boston: Beacon Press.

Hall, C. 1965. Attitudes toward life and death in poetry. *Psychoanalytic Review, 2*: 67–83.

Hall, G.S. 1922. *Senescence*. New York: Appleton-Century-Crofts.

Harms, F. 1941. Child art as an aid in the diagnosis of juvenile neuroses. *American Journal of Orthopsychiatry, 11*: 191–200.

Harnik, J. 1930. One component of the fear of death in early infancy. *International Journal of Psychoanalysis, 2*: 485–491.

Harris, D. 1963. *Children: Drawings as measures of intellectual maturity*. New York: Harcourt, Brace, Jovanovich.

Harrison, S.; Davenport, C.; and McDermott, J. 1967. Children's reactions to bereavement. *Archives of General Psychiatry, 16*: 593–597.

Hebb, D.O. 1949. *The organization of behavior*. New York: John Wiley and Sons.

Hetherington, E.M. 1966. Effects of parental absence on sex-typed behaviors in Negro and white preadolescent males. *Journal of Personality and Social Psychology*, 4: 87–91.

Hetherington, E.M. 1972. Effects of father absence on personality development in adolescent daughters. *Developmental Psychology*, 7: 313–326.

Hevner, K. 1935. Experimental studies of the affective value of colors and lines. *Journal of Applied Psychology*, 19: 385–398.

Hilgard, J.R.; Newman, M.R.; and Fisk, F. 1960. Strength of adult ego following childhood bereavement. *American Journal of Orthopsychiatry*, 30: 788–798.

Hinton, J. 1967. *Dying*. Baltimore: Penguin books.

Hoffman, I. and Futterman, E.H. 1971. Coping with waiting: Psychiatric intervention and study in the waiting room of a pediatric oncology clinic. *Comprehensive Psychiatry*, 1: 67–81.

Huang, I. and Lee, H.W. 1945. Experimental analysis of children's animism. *Journal of Genetic Psychology*, 66: 69–74.

Hurlock, E.B. 1968. *Developmental Psychology* (3rd edition). New York: McGraw-Hill.

Jahoda, G. 1958. Child animism: A critical survey of cross-cultural research. *Journal of Social Psychology*, 47: 213–222.

Jackson, E. 1965. *Telling a child about death*. New York: Chamel Press.

Jung, C.G. 1977. *Memories, dreams, reflections*. Glasgow: Collins-Fountain Books.

Kane, B. 1975. Children's concepts of death. Unpublished doctoral dissertation. University of Cincinnati.

Kanous, L.; Daugherty, R.A.; and Cohn, T.S. 1962. Relation between heterosexual friendship choices and socioeconomic level. *Child Development*, 33: 251–255.

Karon, M. and Vernick, J. 1968. An approach to the emotional support of fatally ill children. *Clinical Pediatrics*, 7: 274–280.

Kastenbaum, R. 1959. Time and death in adolescence. In *The meaning of death*, ed. H. Fiefel, pp. 99–113. New York: McGraw-Hill.

Kastenbaum, R. 1961. The dimensions of future time perspectives: An experimental approach. *Journal of Genetic Psychology, 65:* 203–218.

Kastenbaum, R. 1977. *Death, society and human experience.* St. Louis: C.V. Mosby Co.

Kastenbaum, R. and Aisenberg, R.B. 1972. *The psychology of death.* New York: Springer Publishing Co.

Katzaroff, M.D. 1910. What do children draw? *Archives of Psychology, 9:* 125.

Kavanaugh, R.E. 1972. *Facing death.* Baltimore, Maryland: Penguin Books.

Kelman, H. 1960. Kairos and the therapeutic process. *Journal of Existential Psychiatry, 1:* 233–269.

Kerschensteiner, D.G. 1905. *The development of drawing talent.* Munich: Gerber.

Klein, M. et al. 1952. *Developments in psychoanalysis.* London: The Hogarth Press.

Klingberg, G. 1957. The distribution between living and not living among 7–10 year old children with some remarks concerning the so-called animism controversy. *Journal of Genetic Psychology, 105:* 227–238.

Knudson, A.G. and Natterson, J.M. 1960. Participation of parents in the hospital care of their fatally ill children. *Pediatrics, 26:* 482–490.

Koocher, G. 1973. Childhood, death and cognitive development. *Developmental Psychology, 9:* 369–375.

Kotsovsky, D. 1939. Die psychologie der tudesfurcht (Psychology of the fear of death). *Psychological Abstracts, 13:* 134.

Kübler-Ross, E. 1969. *On death and dying.* New York: MacMillan.

Lark-Horowitz, B. and Norton, J. 1960. Children's art abilities: The interrelations and factorial structure of ten characteristics. *Child Development, 31:* 453–462.

Larson, O.N.; Gray, L.N.; and Fortis, J.G. 1968. Achieving goals through violence on television. *Violence and the Mass Media,* ed. O.N. Larson. New York: Harper and Row.

Lenneberg, E.H. 1964. Speech as a motor skill with special reference to monophasic disorders. In *The Acquisition of Language,* eds. V. Belugi and R. Brown. Monograph of the Society for Research in Child Development, *29:* 162.

Le Shan, E. 1976. *Learning to say goodbye.* New York: Macmillan.

Lessing, G.E. *Wie die alten den tod gebildet (How the ancients represented death).* Leipzig: Reclam, *4:* 172–221.

Lifton, R.J. 1973. The sense of immortality: On death and the continuity of life. *American Journal of Psychoanalysis, 33:* 3–15.

Lonetto, R. 1978. The life-line exercise. Unpublished paper.

Lonetto, R.; Fleming, S.; Gorman, M.; and Best, S. 1975. The psychology of death: A course description with some student perceptions. *Ontario Psychologist, 7*(2): 9–14.

Lonetto, R.; Fleming, S.; Gorman, M.; and Clare, M. 1976. The perceived sex of death and concerns about death. *Essence, 1*(1): 45–58.

Lonetto, R.; Fleming, S.; and Mercer, W. 1979. The structure of death anxiety: A factor analytic study. *Journal of Personality Assessment, 43,4:* 388–392.

Lowenfeld, V. 1952. *Creative and mental growth.* New York: Mac-Millan.

Lundholm, H. 1921. The affective tone of lines: Experimental researches. *Psychological Review, 8:* 43–60.

Maitland, L. 1895. What children draw to please themselves. *Inland Educator, 1:* 187.

Marcovitz, E. 1973. What is the meaning of death to the dying person and his survivors? *Omega, 4:* 13–25.

Marino, D. 1956. Infantile drawings and sexuality. *Psychological Abstracts, 31:* 678.

Markusen, E. and Fulton, R. 1971. Childhood bereavement and behavior disorders: A critical review. *Omega, 2:* 107–117.

Martin, W.E. and Damrin, D.E. 1951. An analysis of the reliability and factorial composition of ratings of children's drawings. *Child Development, 22:* 133–144.

Maurer, A. 1964. Adolescent attitudes towards death. *Journal of Genetic Psychology, 105:* 75–90.

Maurer, A. 1966. Maturation of concepts of death. *British Journal of Medicine and Psychology, 39:* 35–41.

McClelland, D. 1963. The harlequin complex. In *The study of lives,* ed. R. White, pp. 94–119. New York: Atherton Press.

McConville, G.J. et al. 1970. Mourning processes in children of varying ages. *Canadian Psychiatric Association Journal, 5:* 353–355.

McCully, R.S. 1963. Fantasy productions of children with progressively crippling and fatal illness. *Journal of Genetic Psychology, 102:* 203–216.

McFee, J. 1961. *Preparation for art.* San Francisco: Wadsworth.

Minuchin, P. 1965. Sex-role concepts and sex-typing in childhood as a function of school and home environments. *Child Development, 36:* 1033–1048.

Mitchell, M.E. 1967. *The child's attitudes to death.* New York: Schocken Books.

Monsour, J. 1960. Asthma and the fear of death. *Psychoanalytic Quarterly, 29:* 56–71.

Moody, R.A., Jr. 1976. *Life after life.* Atlanta: Mockingbird Books.

Moriarity, D. 1967. *The loss of loved ones.* Springfield, Ill.: Charles C Thomas.

Morrissey, J.R. 1963. Children's adaptations to fatal illness. *Social Work, 8:* 81–88.

Mott, S.M. 1954. Concept of mother: A study of four and five year old children. *Child Development, 25:* 99–106.

Munro, A. 1966. Parental deprivation in depressive patients. *British Journal of Psychiatry, 112:* 443–457.

Munro, A. and Griffiths, A.B. 1969. Some psychiatric non-sequelae of childhood bereavement. *British Journal of Psychiatry, 115:* 305–311.

Nagy, M. 1948. The child's theories concerning death. *Journal of Genetic Psychology, 73:* 3–27.

Natterson, J.M. and Knudson, A.G., Jr. 1960. Observations concerning fear of death in fatally ill children and their mothers. *Psychosomatic Medicine, 22:* 456–465.

Nunally, J. 1967. *Psychometric theory.* New York: McGraw-Hill.

Oltman, J.E.; McGarry, J.J.; and Friedman, S. 1952. Parental deprivation and the broken home in dementia praecox and other mental disorders. *American Journal of Psychiatry, 108:* 685–694.

Osis, K. 1961. *Death-bed observations by physicians and nurses.* New York: Parapsychology Foundation.

Paris, J. and Goodstein, L.D. 1966. Responses to death and sex stimulus materials as a function of repression sensitization. *Psychological Reports, 3:* 1283–1291.

Penfield, W. and Roberts, L. 1958. *Speech and brain mechanisms.* Princeton, N.J.: Princeton University Press.

Piaget, J. 1932. *The moral judgment of the child.* New York: Harcourt, Brace and World, Inc.

Piaget, J. 1952a. *The language and thought of the child.* London: Routledge and Kegan Paul.

Piaget, J. 1952b. *The origins of intelligence in children.* New York: International Universities Press.

Piaget, J. 1954. *The construction of reality in the child.* New York: Basic Books.

Piaget, J. 1959. *Judgment and reasoning in the child.* Paterson, N.J.: Littlefield, Adams and Co.

Piaget, J. 1960. *The child's conception of the world.* Paterson, N.J.: Littlefield, Adams and Co.

Piaget, J. 1966. *The child's conception of physical causality*. London: Routledge and Kegan Paul.

Pitts, F.N.: Meyer, J.; Brooks, M.; and Winokur, G. 1965. Adult psychiatric illness assessed for childhood parental loss and psychiatric illness in family members. *American Journal of Psychiatry, 121:* Suppl., i–x.

Portz, A.T. 1965. The meaning of death to children. *Dissertation Abstracts, 25:* 7383–7384.

Prugh, D.G.; Staub, E.M.; Sands, H.H.; Kirschbaum, R.M.; and Lenihan, E.A. 1953. A study of the emotional responses of children and families to hospitalization and illness. *American Journal of Orthopsychiatry, 23:* 70–106.

Rains, S. and Morris, R. December 1969. The role of the primary teacher in character education. *Young Child, 25:* 105.

Rank, D. 1958. *Beyond psychology*. New York: Dover Press.

Read, H. 1945. *Education through art*. New York: Pantheon Books.

Reichenberg-Hackett, W. 1953. Changes in Goodenough's drawings after a gratifying experience. *American Journal of Orthopsychiatry, 23:* 501–517.

Rilke, R.M. 1961. *Sämtliche werke (Complete works)*. Frankfort: Insel Verlag, 4: 357–367.

Rochlin, G. 1953. *Loss and restitution: The psychoanalytic study of the child*, pp. 288–309. New York: International Universities Press.

Rochlin, G. 1967. How younger children view death and themselves. In *Explaining death to children*, ed. E.A. Grollman. Boston: Beacon Press.

Rosenblatt, B. 1967. Reactions of children to the death of loved ones: Some notes based on psychoanalytic theory. In *The loss of loved ones*, ed. D.M. Moriarity, pp. 135–145. Springfield, Ill.: Charles C Thomas.

Ross, R.P. 1967. Separation fear and the fear of death in children. *Dissertation Abstracts International, 27:* 2878–2879.

Rouma, G. 1913. *The child's graphic language*. Paris: Mischel et Thron.

Safier, G. 1964. A study in relationships between the life and death concepts in children. *Journal of Genetic Psychology, 105:* 283–294.

Schachter, S. 1959. *The psychology of affiliation.* Stanford, Calif.: Stanford University Press.

Scheerer, M. and Lyons, J. 1947. Line drawing and matching responses to words. *Journal of Personality, 25:* 251–273.

Schilder, P. and Levine, E.L. 1942. Abstract art as an expression of human problems. *Journal of Nervous and Mental Disorders, 95:* 1–10.

Schilder, P. and Wechsler, D. 1934. The attitudes of children toward death. *Journal of Genetic Psychology, 45:* 406–451.

Schowalter, J.E. 1970. The child's reaction to his own terminal illness. In *Psychological management in medical practice,* eds. B. Schoenberg, A. Carr, D. Peretz, and A. Kutscher. New York: Columbia University Press.

Schur, T.J. 1971. What man has told children about death. *Omega,* 2: 84–90.

Scott, C.A. 1896. Old age and death. *American Journal of Psychology, 8:* 67–122.

Seeman, E. 1934. Development of the pictorial aptitude in children. *Character and Personality, 2:* 209–221.

Shambaugh, B. 1961. A study of loss reactions in a seven-year-old boy. *The Psychoanalytic Study of the Child, 16:* 510–522.

Shapiro, D.S. 1957. Perceptions of significant family and environmental relationships in aggressive and withdrawn children. *Journal of Consulting Psychology, 21:* 381–385.

Sharl, A. 1961. Regression and restitution in object loss. *Psychoanalytic Study of the Child, 16:* 471–480.

Sherman, L.J. 1958. Sexual differentiation or artistic ability? *Journal of Clinical Psychology, 14:* 170–171.

Shirley, M. and Goodenough, F.L. 1932. A survey of the intelligence of deaf children in Minnesota schools. *American Annals of the Deaf, 77:* 238–247.

Shoor, M. and Speed, M.H. 1963. Death, delinquency, and the mourning process. *Psychiatric Quarterly, 37:* 540–558.

Singer, D.B. 1970. Violence, protest and war in television news: The U.S. and Canada compared. *Public Opinion Quarterly, 34:* 611–616.

Skonsen, W.C. 1962. *So you want to raise a boy.* New York: Doubleday.

Slater, P.E. 1963. The face of death. Unpublished manuscript. Framingham, Mass.: Cushing Hospital.

Spinetta, J.J. 1974. The dying child's awareness of death. *Psychological Bulletin, 4:* 256–260.

Spinetta, J.J.: Rigler, D.; and Karon, M. 1973. Anxiety in the dying child. *Pediatrics, 52:* 127–131.

Stein, M. 1955. *The thematic apperception test: An introductory manual for its clinical use with adults.* Cambridge, Mass.: Addison-Wesley Publishing Co., Inc.

Steiner, G.L. 1965. Children's concepts of life and death: A developmental study. *Dissertation abstracts international, 26:* 1164.

Stewart, L.H. 1955. The expression of personality in drawings and paintings. *Genetic Psychological Monographs, 51:* 45–103.

Stotijn-Egge, S. 1952. *Investigation of the drawing ability of low-grade oligophrenics.* Leiden: Luctor et Emergo.

Strang, R. 1959. *An introduction to child study.* New York: MacMillan.

Suzuki, D.T. 1963. *Outlines of Mahayana Buddhism.* New York: Schocken Books.

Swensen, C.N. and Newton, K.R. 1955. The development of sexual differentiation on the Draw-A-Person test. *Journal of Clinical Psychology, 11:* 417–419.

Swenson, W.M. 1961. Attitudes toward death in an aged population. *Journal of Gerontology, 16:* 49–52.

Tallmer, M.: Fornanck, R.; and Tallmer, J. 1974. Factors influencing children's concepts of death. *Journal of Clinical Child Psychology, 3:* 17–19.

Templer, D.I. 1976. Two-factor theory of death anxiety: A note. *Essence*, 1(2): 91–94.

Vernick, J. and Lunceford, J.L. March 1967. Milieu design for adolescents with leukemia. *American Journal of Nursing*, 3: 222–224.

Vernon, G.M. and Payne, W.D. 1973. Myth conceptions about death. *Journal of Religion and Health*, 12: 63–76.

Von Hug Hellmuth, H. 1965. The child's concept of death. *Psychoanalytic Quarterly*, 34: 499–516.

Vygotsky, L. 1962. *Thought and language*. Cambridge, Mass.: M.I.T. Press.

Wachner, T. 1946. Interpretation of spontaneous drawings and paintings. *Genetic Psychological Monographs*, 33: 3–70.

Waechter, E.H. 1971. Children's awareness of fatal illness. *American Journal of Nursing*, 71: 1168–1172.

Wahl, C.W. 1959. The fear of death. In *The meaning of death*, ed. H. Fiefel. New York: McGraw-Hill.

Watson, E.J. and Lowrey, G.J. 1958. *Growth and development of children*. Chicago: Year Book Medical Publishers.

Watts, A. 1964. *Beyond theology*. New York: Vintage Books.

Watts, A. 1973. *Psychotherapy East and West*. New York: Ballantine Books.

Weider, A. and Noller, P.A. 1953. Objective studies of children's drawings of human figures, II: Sex, age, intelligence. *Journal of Clinical Psychology*, 9: 20–23.

Wheeler, L. 1970. *Interpersonal influence*. Boston: Allyn and Bacon.

Whorf, B. 1956. *Language, thought and reality*. New York: John Wiley and Sons.

Wohlwill, J.F. and Wiener, M. 1964. Discrimination of form orientation in young children. *Child Development*, 35: 1113–1125.

Wolf, A.M. 1973. *Helping your child to understand death*. New York: Child Study Press.

Wolfenstein, M. 1951. The emergence of fun morality. *Journal of Social Issues, 7:* 15–25.

Wolff, W. 1946. *The personality of the preschool child: The child's search for his self.* New York: Grune and Stratton.

Yochelson, L., ed. 1967. *Symposium on suicide.* Washington, D.C.: George Washington University Press.

Zilboorg, G. 1943. Fear of death. *Psychoanalytic Quarterly, 12:* 465–475.

Additional Readings

Baggett, A.T. 1967. The effect of early loss of father upon the personality of boys and girls in late adolescence. *Dissertation Abstracts, 28:* (1–B): 356–357.

Bendiksen, R. and Fulton, R. 1975. Death and the child: An anterospective test of the childhood bereavement and later behavior disorder hypothesis. *Omega, 6:* 45–49.

Biorck, G. August 1967. Thoughts on life and death. Paper presented at the First World Meeting on Medical Law in Ghent, Belgium.

Boulding, K. 1956. *The image.* Ann Arbor, Michigan: University of Michigan Press.

Bozeman, M.F.; Orbach, G.E.; and Sutherland, A.M. 1955. Psychological impact of cancer and its treatment—adaptation of mothers to the threatened loss of their child through leukemia: I. *Cancer, 8:* 1–19.

Bridges, K.M.B. 1932. Emotional development in early infancy. *Child Development, 3:* 324–341.

Dennehy, C. 1966. Childhood bereavement and psychiatric illness. *British Journal of Psychiatry, 112:* 1049–1069.

Dennis, W. 1934. A description and classification of the responses of the newborn. *Psychological Bulletin, 31:* 5–22.

Fast, I. and Cain, A.C. 1966. The stepparent role: Potential for disturbances in family functioning. *American Journal of Orthopsychiatry, 36:* 485–491.

Forrest, A.D.; Fraser, R.H.; and Priest, R.G. 1965. Environmental factors in depressive illness. *British Journal of Psychiatry, 111:* 243–253.

Fraisse, P. 1959. *The psychology of time.* New York: Harper Torchbooks.

Gorer, G. 1965a. *Death, grief, and mourning.* New York: Doubleday.

Gorer, G. 1965b. *The pornography of death.* In *Identity and Anxiety,* eds. M. Stein, A. Vidich, and D.M. White, pp. 402–407. New York: Free Press.

Greer, S. 1964. Study of parental loss in neurotics and sociopaths. *Archives of General Psychiatry, 11:* 177–180.

Gregory, I. 1958. Studies of parental deprivation in psychiatric patients. *American Journal of Psychiatry, 115:* 423–432.

Gregory, I. 1965. Anterospective data following childhood loss of a parent. *Archives of General Psychiatry, 13:* 99–109.

Gruenberg, S.M., ed. 1952. *Our children today.* New York: The Viking Press.

Harnovitch, M.B. 1964. *The parent and the fatally ill child.* Los Angeles: Delmar Press.

Hilgard, J. and Newman, M. 1963. Early parental deprivation in schizophrenia and alcoholism. *American Journal of Orthopsychiatry, 3:* 409–420.

Hill, O.W. and Price, J.S. 1967. Childhood bereavement and adult depression. *British Journal of Psychiatry, 113:* 743–751.

Hite, K.E. November 19, 1968. A phenomenon of rebirth: Coming alive in analytic and medical patients. Paper presented to the Association for the Advancement of Psychoanalysis at the New York Academy of Medicine.

Hopkinson, G. and Reed, G.F. 1966. Bereavement in childhood and depressive psychosis. *British Journal of Psychiatry, 112:* 459–463.

Howell, D.A. February, 1967. A child dies. *Hospital Topics.*

Huang, I. 1943. Children's conceptions of physical causality: A critical summary. *Journal of Genetic Psychology, 63:* 71–121.

Ingram, H.V. 1949. A statistical study of family relationships in psychoneurosis. *American Journal of Psychiatry, 106:* 91–100.

Irwin, O.C. 1930. The amount and nature of activities of newborn infants under constant conditions during the first ten days of life. *Genetic Psychological Monographs, 8:* 1–92.

Kaess, L.R. August 1971. Death as an event: A commentary on Robert Morison. *Science, 173:* 698–702.

Kastenbaum, R. July 1966. As the clock runs out. *Mental Hygiene, 50:* 332–336.

Kliman, G. 1968. *Psychological emergencies of childhood.* New York: Grune and Stratton.

Kliman, G. 1969. The child faces his own death. In *Death and Bereavement,* ed. A.H. Kutscher, pp. 20–27. Springfield, Ill.: Charles C Thomas.

Lidz, R. and Lidz, T. 1949. Family environment of schizophrenic patients. *American Journal of Psychiatry, 106:* 332–345.

Lynn, D.B. 1974. *The father: His role in child development.* Monterey, Calif.: Brooks/Cole.

Lystad, M. 1959. Childhood and adult family structure of schizophrenic patients. *Diseases of the Nervous System, 20:* 57–62.

Mauer, A. 1961. A child's knowledge of non-existence. *Journal of Existential Psychiatry, 2:* 193–212.

May, R. 1950. *The meaning of anxiety.* New York: Ronald Press.

Medawar, P.B. 1957. *The uniqueness of the individual.* New York: Basic Books.

Morison, R.S. August 1971. Death: Process or event. *Science, 3998:* 173.

Pollock, G.H. 1962. Childhood parent and sibling loss in adult patients. *Archives of General Psychiatry, 7:* 87–97.

Richmond, J.B. and Warsman, H.A. 1955. Psychological aspects of management of children with malignant diseases. *American Journal of Diseases of the Child, 89:* 42–47.

Rochlin, G. 1961. *The dread of abandonment,* pp. 451–470. In the Psychoanalytic Study of the Child. New York: International Universities Press.

Rochlin, G. 1965. *Griefs and discontents.* Boston: Little, Brown and Co.

Sabatini, P. and Kastenbaum, R. 1973. The do-it-yourself death certificate as a research technique. *Life-threatening behavior, 3:* 20–32.

Sciarra, L. February 1967. Problem in the dying patient with a fatal neurological illness. Paper presented at Conference on Care of Patients, New York Academy of Sciences, New York, N.Y.

Simpson, M.A. 1979. *The facts of death,* Englewood Cliffs, N.J.: Prentice Hall.

Wahl, C.W. 1954. Some antecedent factors in the family histories of 392 schizophrenics. *American Journal of Psychiatry, 110:* 668–676.

Wahl, C.W. 1956. Some antecedent factors in the family histories of 568 male schizophrenics in the United States Navy. *American Journal of Psychiatry, 113:* 201–209.

Weisman, A.D. and Hackett, T.P. 1961. Predilection to death: Death and dying as a psychiatric problem. *Psychosomatic Medicine, 23:* 232–256.

Wilson, I.C.; Alltop, L.B.; and Buffaloe, W.J. 1967. Parental bereavement in childhood: M.M.P.I. profiles in a depressed population. *British Journal of Psychiatry, 113:* 761–764.

NAME INDEX

SUBJECT INDEX